Flip the Switch

by Michelle Mueller

Flip the Switch
By Michelle Mueller

ISBN: 978-0-9998189-3-0

Edited by Eli Gonzalez and Lil Barcaski
Book Design by Ymmy Marketing LLC

For information address inquiries to:
www.theghostpublishing.com

Printed in USA

Dedication:

This book is a tribute to the men and women that fought and died to defend the freedoms and advantages we experience in this country today. I am proud to be an AMERICAN. I feel greatly privileged to have the opportunity to raise our children in the legendary U.S.A. There is nowhere else in the world where one can quit a job they hate one day and become their own boss the next. The highest praise to the American entrepreneurial spirit and the men and women that protect it!

Foreword

Kevin Harrington was an original "shark" on the hit TV show Shark Tank. His legendary work behind-the-scenes of business ventures has produced well over $5 billion in global sales, the launch of more than 500 products, and the making dozens of millionaires. Twenty of his companies have each topped $100 million in revenue. For more than 30 years, Kevin Harrington has been a success catalyst, empowering entrepreneurs and innovative business leaders to turn dreams into mind-boggling reality.

Shark Tank – *Why do 300 ideas get chosen from 50,000 submissions?*

Simple, they have the infrastructure to be a force on the global level.

I love the American entrepreneurial spirit and trust me, it is not dead. I love when someone comes up with a new and bright idea that has real possibilities and when that person has the tenacity to bring it to life. I've seen many businesses come and go and I've found that passion is what often is the key factor to success.

I receive hundreds of business opportunities every single month and very few of them grab me. But one that particularly caught my eye was Garden Light LED and their Master Dealer Program. Without question this program will bring out the entrepreneur in you. It was engineered to allow eligible lighting design dealers to double or triple their businesses in two to three years. Garden Lighting LED is the rocket ship you want to hitch yourself to if you want your business to go to the next level in the lighting space

The tools to success are all there: A great American built outdoor LED product line; engineering that is Swiss inspired; comprehensive hands-on training by the best engineers & installers in the industry; and, last but not least, a game-changing sales and digital marketing strategy that is designed for Dealers to dominate their local LED markets.

This book will take you step by step through how Michelle and Reto built their amazing business and show you how you can be part of the Garden Light LED family. These are self-made entrepreneurs who are paving a path for success for the companies that become part of their Master Dealer Program. The most important things you need before you read this book are, a willingness to learn about the power of digital marketing, and a belief that anyone can become successful in the lighting design business if they're willing to hustle and follow the program. Some of the success stories you will read here are of people that had no background in this industry at all but simply had the drive, determination and follow-through of an entrepreneur.

One thing you must understand, and embrace is that the future of retail is changing. It's going to be a combination of eCommerce with Digital Currency. The proof is vast and widely available; just open your eyes. If you are an Entrepreneur looking to make your mark, you should be looking at what many of the successful companies like: Amazon, eBay, Google and Facebook have done for the last ten years in the online space. These companies are dominating the marketplace; why, because of the platforms they created, which yields the ability to go to the public.

There are three things an entrepreneur needs to do to compete in today's marketplace:

Discover

Look for an idea that solves a problem; eases the pain; or one that improves upon an existing business model. How do you know if your idea or product accomplishes that?

Test before you invest.

We have all heard of Alpha and Beta testing; now, embrace it. Figure out where improvements can be made ahead of time; therefore, protecting yourself from spending a ton of money in the future to "fix" broken strategies.

Demonstrate

Demonstrate the product by creating the perfect pitch. The lack of accomplishing this is where people fell-down on Shark Tank.

This is a 3-pronged effort:

- *Tease:* Grab the audience with something that gets their attention and makes them fall in love with the idea or product.

- *Please:* Show the benefits. How will this solve a problem, improve their lives, make them happy.

- *Seize:* Ask for a buying action. Don't be afraid to ask for the sale. ABC: Always Be Closing.

Dominate

Learning as much from failures as you do from success is key. Be prepared for stumbles; be prepared for ups and downs. Life's battles are not always won by the fastest or the strongest; they're more often won by those who believe they can win.

With the proper plan, the main objective is for entrepreneurs to go from an idea to an empire.

Garden Light LED's modern business model is: "We're not in the lighting business serving people; we're in the people business serving lighting." That's a fantastic way to look at any business that serves the public.

All-in-all, the entrepreneurial vision is kept alive by expecting better every day. This attitude will catapult a great idea into an empire. And, as always, follow the golden rule in business - to persevere no matter what challenges are ahead.

I hope you enjoy the book. I hope it challenges you to up your game and become part of the new American entrepreneurial landscape.

Table of Contents

Introduction

The American Dream. Many have sought it, fought for it, some thought they had it and lost it, and others feel it's been long dead. Yet, not only is it alive, in certain verticals, it's thriving!

The main reason why I absolutely, positively love what I do is because I help talented, driven people obtain the great American Dream of Business Ownership. It is extremely gratifying for me to light the pathway of professional independence for those courageous enough to seek it. I love that I help people of all walks of life, races, religions, and education levels, become successful business owners.

I travel all over these United States of North America and meet landscapers, LED lighting professionals, architects, manufacturer reps, and people who can't shake their entrepreneurial spirit, and show them how to capture the oftentimes fleeting dream of working for themselves.

At the end of the day, when all is said and done, I don't think there are many better things one can say about someone else other than their lives have been greatly improved by knowing him or her.

My company, Garden Lighting LED has been in business for more than two decades. We have encountered the screwiest, zaniest issues and have reached milestones we never thought we could when we started. There is no way we could have done what we've done alone. We have been fortunate to provide financial stability for numerous employees that treat our company as their own. We have formed relationships with our employees, and their families that extend far beyond the working hours of the day. Occasionally, I still get a heartfelt thank you for providing someone a job. It's a humbling, yet great feeling to know that I've helped many families.

I'm honored to say that doesn't just end with our employees and their families, by offering our Master Dealer program, we've shown people from all over the country how to not only run a lighting company, but how to do so and dominate their market. I enjoy taking on the challenge of helping someone start a new business or working alongside someone who has an existing landscaping business and partnering with them. We allow them to do what they're good at and provide unparalleled support in other areas that they may not have expertise in such as digital marketing or driving traffic to their website.

The end result of hiring people and partnering with business owners across the country is found in the stellar products we help deliver to our end users; home owners, business owners, and commercial property owners. We have received many testimonials over the years:

"We love our house!"

"We can finally entertain"

"We feel much safer now"

Some have even said, they can't live without it!

What most people don't know is that colors trigger subliminal messages to the brain. *(More on the psychological effects of color in the book)*. I truly believe that the right lighting (color schemes, angles, ambiances, etc.) increases people's quality of life and adds years to their lives.

The reason why I champion the American Dream is because someone like me was never supposed to realize it. I grew up on the streets of East Detroit. My parents divorced when I was three. While my mother gave me all the support she could, she worked often and the only other person at home was my brother who is five years older. I became self-driven at an early age to make something of myself. My plan was to go to college but that never happened.

I was fortunate to start modelling modeling at the age of 18. Model for the bridal campaign, swam in a shark tank for the Florida Aquarium ad campaigns, starred in a Tropicana commercial, and was an HSN on-air model and eventually helped sell products on air for vendors. I was involved in many large-scale productions where many people had to do a variety of tasks. Like a sponge, I soaked up the knowledge on how production managers influenced others in order to deliver a high-quality and successful campaigns. By the time I met Reto, my husband, life partner, and business partner, I had acquired management and team building skills that complimented his drive and experience in the lighting industry.

Reto has been in the trenches, he's dug ditches, he's offered free lighting installations... he did whatever it took to showcase the quality of our products. We know what it takes to build a lucrative business; the good, the bad, and the ugly. Since we found our groove, we've shared our knowledge and partnered with hundreds of American entrepreneurs for over two decades. To date, we have helped thirty businesses become multi-million-dollar companies!

I hope this book falls into the hands of those people who feel trapped in their jobs or who feel their business has hit a ceiling. There are millions of people who would love to own their own lucrative business. If you are one of those that want to work for yourself, maybe you hate your boss, or have a sliver of an inclination to achieve the American dream of business ownership and financial independence – I wrote this book for you!

I've helped people build multi-million-dollar businesses in the lighting industry. We are certified experts and thought leaders. I wrote this book to spark hope in you that manifests itself into partnership with us. I want to help you grow your business. I want you to expand your product offerings. I want you to focus on the things you are great at and support you in areas where we can help. I've gone through heartache and triumph and through my experiences, I can shed light on the oftentimes dark road of successful business ownership.

The story of your life has yet to be written. I challenge you to enter into a new chapter in your life. Read this book and find out how to achieve the American dream. Dare to leave a legacy for your children. I'm here to help.

Chapter 1

Our What and Why

By the time you're done reading this book, you're never going to look at the lighting design industry the same way. If there's a sliver of entrepreneurship in your heart, it will grow to the point that it will consume you and catapult you into action.

How do I know? I've done it. This is a success story, and it can be your story as well.

I love the book *Start with Why* by Simon Sinek. In Chapter 8, "Start with Why, but Know with What," *"In every case of a great charismatic leader who ever achieved anything of significance, there was always a person or small group lurking in the shadows who knew the HOW to take the vision and make it a reality. Martin Luther King had Ralph Abernathy, Bill Gates Visionary had Paul Allen and Steve Ballmer."*

"Walt Disney dreamed, drew and imagined, his brother Roy Disney stayed in the shadow forming an empire," wrote Bob Thomas, a Disney biographer. In nearly every case of a person or an organization that has gone onto inspire people and do great things, there exists this special partnership between WHY and HOW. That's how it is with Reto and I. We are the Why and How for each other. He's my partner in business and in life. We teeter-totter back and forth; one taking the lead as the visionary with an innovative idea that the other helps execute and then the other way around. Our strengths rise as needed. We are both Yin and Yang, which makes for a truly successful partnership; like Walt and Roy, only we are both Walt, and we are both Roy. It just depends on who has an idea worth pursuing next.

One of my all-time favorite innovators is, of course, Steve Jobs. He was the rebel evangelist, but Steve Wozniak is the engineer who made the Apple work. Jobs had the vision, Woznaik had the goods, it is a partnership of the vision, of the future, and the talent to get it done. Another great partnership was that of Herb Kelleher and Rollin King. Herb was all about freedom and wanted to give people a way to fly anywhere they wanted to go without charging exorbitant amounts of money. He dreamed of an airline that would give the public freedom of movement, but it was Rollin King who came up with the idea of Southwest Airlines. He was a man who wouldn't let up. Like Jobs, he too wanted to make a dent in the universe and so do I.

They say passion doesn't always make you money, but I don't believe that. I run on passion and it has served me well. My passion has brought me success in business, finances, and life. My greatest passion is sharing what we've learned over 20 years, applying it to other businesses and having them grow and be successful.

The world is full of emerging innovation and we too are innovators. When I see our engineers make a new product that pushes the technology of lighting forward, I know we're on the right path. We're on the cutting edge and it fuels my ever-growing passion for our work, our company and our industry. Garden Light LED has initiated some amazing advances in the lighting industry. It's hard to believe how far we've come and we're just getting started from our beginning as a 3-person company, box in box out, reseller to a full-blown, American manufacturing facility. Today we have a clean room, production room, engineering department, and Haas CNC and mill machines. We turn our own metal, do rapid prototyping, CAD, solid works, and 3-d printing. We even create our own light engines and drivers and have a full testing and warranty facility.

Very few manufacturers are doing this. Bringing all this in house was neither cheap nor easier. Now add into this the fact that we are instructing others, helping them build their businesses so that our great technology is put out into the world.

Our products are all American, made by American workers in the heart of Florida's Sunbelt. We make outstanding, unique products that can compete, not only in quality, but in price with anything on the market today. That's great and we're proud of our work, but we have one more edge that puts us miles ahead of the competition. Digital Marketing is the future and with the addition of our expert digital marketing service, we can't be beat. We're going to explain this concept in this book and we will get to that.

But why should you believe me? How did we get to this place and why do we want to share our knowledge and experience with you? Why do we want to make you more successful? What's in it for us?

People do business with people they know, like and trust. As Kevin told you in his forward, we're not in the lighting business serving people; we're in the people business serving lighting." The people we serve are not the end client as much as they are the lighting designers, installers, contractors, landscapers, architects, even the person that just left the military and is looking for a real opportunity. We've helped people from all walks of life build and grow a business that they can be proud of; one that feeds their family and gives them a quality lifestyle. All they had to do was believe in themselves and our program and be willing to do the work.

People looking to buy a franchise, without a franchise fee, who are looking for a high-quality, wildly-desired product they can make a good margin on are strong candidates for this program.

Reto and Michelle

So, who are we and how did we get here?

My husband and I come from very different places in the world, yet there are so many touch points that made our connection inevitable. I was born in Michigan and, until the age of 10, grew up on the fast streets of East Detroit, surrounded by factory workers and a world where innovation ruled. Ford, Chrysler, General Motors were all there. Manufacturing is in my blood.

Detroit was struggling in the 1980's. Japanese cars were smaller and more economic and the Big 3 were pushing hard to win back the American public. Lee Iacocca took over Chrysler around that time. Before that, he had been at Ford and developed the Mustang and Pinto. Iacocca was a passionate advocate of U.S. business exports during the 1980s. He believed in the idea of Made in America and knew that had value in the rest of the world. He was one of the innovators that was keeping Detroit alive and kicking. I was just a kid then, but I remember Detroit as a vibrant and exciting, albeit tough, place to live.

> They say passion doesn't always make you money, but I don't believe that. I run on passion and it has served me well.

My father was an engineer in the auto industry, but he and my mother divorced when I was three years old. I lived with my mom, who had two jobs, and my older brother. She worked days in a Kroger's grocery store manning the deli and at night as a server in a Mexican restaurant.

At that age I learned very quickly to take care of myself. What choice was there? My brother thought it was funny to try and make me cry but I was a tough cookie; self-sufficient and not a cry baby. I had street smarts early on and no matter what ridiculous thing he'd come up with, I never cracked.

Despite my being the younger sibling, I was hyper-protective of him, constantly looking out for him. All I wanted was for everyone to be safe. So long as everyone was good, I was good. My brother was very important to me. My mom was busy and not around much of the time, so he was the most important person to me. I didn't want to be alone. What if I lost him?

"You make me nervous." I would tell him. "Don't do anything stupid."

We both played sports all our lives, but in Detroit sports meant rivalries. Every township was in hard core competition with the others. The streets were crowded, and kids and teens would duke it out over their sports standings. I was always worried about my brother getting into fights, so I followed him around and did my best to keep him out of harm's way.

When I was ten years old my mom re-married and we moved to Plant City, Florida. Talk about culture shock. Suddenly we lived in a place where there were farms growing everything from oranges to tomatoes and, of course, strawberries. The kids didn't fight on the streets over stickball games and whose sports team was better. They went 4-wheeling and rode dirt bikes, fished in the lakes and ate barbeque. All I can say is, it grew on me. I'm still here in Florida, not far from where I grew up. It's home.

I graduated high school rather young; 17 to be exact and I gave college a try but lasted exactly one semester. I wasn't what you'd call a stellar college student. It seemed pointless to me and I didn't want to waste more time there. Instead, I started modelling, mostly for magazines and ad agencies down in Miami. I landed some big campaigns for companies like Walt Disney World, Tropicana and Marshalls and got into some TV commercials. That led me to the Home Shopping Network as a spokes model and eventually an on-air talent. It seems I was blessed with the personality and the right looks for this kind of work, but the more important thing was that I had determination. Maybe seeing my mother work two jobs to give us a decent life was the lesson I needed to show me a path to my own success. To some degree, it was just the kind of personality I was born with.

I had a way of influencing people at a very young age. I used to do a Minnie Pearl impersonation and get people to laugh. Humor is a great tool and somehow using that would result in getting people to do things my way. Sales came easy to me.

I decided I needed to have a steady job to offset any lulls in the modelling gigs. At 18, I worked in reservations at Alamo Rent-a-Car. It was one of my first jobs and I was a big up-seller, talking guests into bigger cars and adding insurance. In 1993, Hurricane Andrew hit, and I was working in the corporate offices in Miami where many of the clients were Spanish-speaking. Suddenly, we had a rush on car rentals. I guess a lot of people lost their cars in the storm. I didn't speak a word of anything other than English, but I learned how to execute a car rental, in Spanish, by rote. I learned, word for word, how to communicate all the necessary paperwork, options, insurance, and intricacies in a language I had no knowledge of. Turns out necessity *is* the mother of invention. To this day, it's the only Spanish I can speak. I guess it's better than most people's high school Spanish which consists of, "my name is...," and "Where is the bathroom?"

My first big job that led me to where I am now came with some serendipity. When I was 15, I had my first crush on a young man who was quite a bit older than I. Our family sat behind his family in church. I declared my intention, to all my girlfriends, that someday I was going to marry him. But he was too old for me at the time and his lack of interest broke my heart. I had been living in Miami for a while, but moved back to Tampa and one day, as luck would have it, I saw him driving along on the interstate. I honked and waved, and we pulled off the road to talk. Turned out that he owned a magazine called Lawn and Landscape and he was also launching another one called Florida Golf Monthly. He was having great success, but he needed someone to sell advertising. I quickly realized that he had no chemical companies advertising in his lawn and landscape publication. We began dating and I worked for him and had great success with advertising sales. I quickly landed a big account with Dow Chemical. The dating worked out for a while, but ultimately wasn't a good fit for either of us. I eventually broke off the relationship but continued working as an independent contractor and did the majority of the advertising sales for the publications. For the next five years I learned everything there was to know about publishing. I not only sold advertising, I worked on the monthly layout and art direction too. I liked sales and I was good at it, but this was what I really loved; ad layout, printing and the whole creative process of it. I learned all the aspects of producing a monthly publication and what a big undertaking it was. I had no idea at the time how useful these skills would be when I owned my own business. I have been the head of the marketing department for Garden Light LED for the past 15 years, creating our marketing strategy and being hands on in the whole process. Skills I learned from my magazine days. You never know where life will lead you.

I learned to create strategies for getting people to work together who normally didn't. An example of this was a deal I worked out with Anheuser-Busch. They didn't want to advertise in smaller, more local publications like ours as a rule, so I went to the regional distributers and got them to put up half the money for an ad. It was a small amount per distributer, so it didn't break their banks and I got the folks at the corporate level at Anheuser-Busch to match the funds to make up the rest of the cost of advertising; a win-win for all.

Despite my efforts to bring in advertising dollars, the magazines were going into failure. Lack of cooperation among the partners was making it difficult to move in a coherent way.

Around that time, I met Reto and my life took an unexpected and fortuitous turn.

Reto was born in Switzerland and had a very similar life-changing experience to mine. At ten years of age, he was suddenly yanked from the life he knew and moved to (you guessed it) Florida. His mother put them on a DC10 and moved Reto and his two sisters to Madeira Beach to start a new life with a new husband. Reto was traumatized by the move. He was born in a Swiss farmhouse. His father was a farmer and he thought he would follow that path as well. Reto had no idea this move was coming, and he was forced to leave everything he knew behind.

His mother came from extreme wealth. His Grandfather was in manufacturing, which is in Reto's blood as well. His mom's family owned the Cartone Box Company that was started in the 1930's and sold on the stock exchange by the 1960's. Reto's father was a farm boy. When they married,

Reto's mother bought his father a farm with her inheritance. He was young when the relationship soured, but it was a bitter ending and his mother forbade his dad to see their kids. Reto didn't reconnect with his father until he was 18.

Reto is meticulous, a trait that goes back to his born sense of swiss engineering. He loves innovation and knows warehousing. He has what you would call a nose for business. He's downright prescient about what business might take off or what one will be a dud. Like me, he didn't graduate from college. His new father was in the restaurant business and he grew up around that, but it wasn't his calling. Instead, he had an instinct and an affinity for the ceiling fan business. His very first job was with Dan's Fan City. He spent two years trying to get that job and only got a chance at it because someone took ill and they needed a replacement. Reto had been so persistent that they gave him a shot.

He loved it!

Within a very short period, he left Dan's and started his own ceiling fan business, which included a lighting showroom. Soon, he was the top distributer for Casablanca Ceiling fans in the United States. Reto had marketing mojo. To drive sales, he would do things like put a crazy, high price on a couple of ceiling fans and place stanchions around them saying they weren't for sale. Naturally, people would beg to buy them. He instinctively knew the psychology of sales. Like me, he was a natural-born salesperson and entrepreneur. It's simply in the blood.

He was going along gangbusters but started to make some serious mistakes; bad life decisions -and he lost it all. In 1996, he hit rock bottom, got into some legal troubles and spent millions on his own defense. He came out of all of that knowing he had to change his ways. I think he had to go through all that to come out the other side a better man.

He was living in his car when an idea came to him. He has a knack for new markets when they are pre-explosion. A friend of his gave him a $2000 line of credit for lighting and with it he started a lighting design business. He had three lighting products to sell and a lot of gumption. By the time I met him a couple of years later, he had installed over 2,000 lighting fixtures for his customers. People would call him because it was new and trending. He was bringing light to the world and he loved it.

When I met him, I was impressed by his story and his business sense. The magazines were tanking, and he said, "Come work with me." Soon thereafter, I quit my job. Reto had set up shop in Clearwater in a 10x10 executive suite. I fell in love with the lighting business and with him. That was 1999 and by 2001, we had gotten married and moved Garden Light to Tampa to a 2500 square feet facility. I asked my administrative assistant from the publications, Rene Morris to come with us, and she said yes. It was just the three of us for many years and Rene is still with company, now as our administrative manager.

Big Breaks

The first big break we got was a mixture of luck, timing and the genius of my partner. At that time, we sold three light fixtures, all of which were made in Taiwan by one company. We got word that the company was closing its doors. China had entered the market and was making fixtures at a third of the price, so everything was shifting to the Chinese. Reto called the company in Taiwan and, surprisingly, a woman answered the phone and she spoke to him in English, which was even more of a surprise. Reto wasted no time and flew to Taiwan. He helped them get their warehouse and products in order. They had two fixtures we sold a lot of, the F-7150 and the F-777 spotlights and we didn't want to see them go out of business. For the next two weeks, Reto met with them every day to brainstorm. He was able to turn their company around in the two weeks he spent with them and they're still operating today. They already had the UK market and the Asian market but were losing other markets to China. In exchange for helping them stay in business, they gave us exclusive rights to sell their products in America. What they made was a much higher quality product than what was coming out of China. We helped them expand their product line and drive down the cost in doing so. Now we had exclusive rights to a line of much higher quality lights that no one else had and we sold millions of fixtures at $19.99.

The second big break we got was when Reto created a relationship with a guy from Philadelphia who was the largest manufacturer of transformers for lighting displays. He wanted to help us.

"I want to make you a success," he said.

And he did just that. He gave us a big advantage over our competition by giving us a deal on the best-made transformer out there. No small businesses were getting the pricing for this transformer that we were. I started in Tampa by calling contractors. "Have you considered doing outdoor lighting? Have you ever heard of Garden Light?" I would ask each of them these same questions.

"We'd love to add that feature, but we don't know how to do it." I got the same reply nearly all the time. We decided the best path to take was to teach people how to build a lighting design business. The big key for getting contractors involved was getting that better deal on transformers.

For decades, our philosophy was teaching them how to own their own business. We had a small business, low overhead, and made our monthly rent the first two days of any month.

I would simply "dial for dollars. "

"We've got a lifetime warranty," I would tell them. "And we will teach you what you need to know to sell our products."

From 2000-2007 we worked with a lot of installers. My breath is for this contractor community; American entrepreneurship and to raise the level of experience for their customers.

We didn't have much, but we had business acumen. We had passion to sell, passion for the lighting industry and what these products could do for the end user. But without the installers, we had nothing.

We became a supplier for nearly 500 dealers over the ten-year period leading to 2009. We met people along the way that wanted to own their own business; waitresses, hockey coaches, ex-military, airline pilots, travel agents and even the husband of our kids' nanny; people that got what it meant to be an American entrepreneur and that had the right stuff. We were not just building a business, we were building people up.

Then in 2007 the market crashed. But we were, and still are, a debt-free, profitable company. We don't have receivables. With us, you pay up front. Our clients work on a higher profit margin. If you can't afford to do business with us, we can't afford doing business with you.

In 2009 LED lighting hit the market. And that's when the real fun started.

Chapter 2

LED Lighting Takes Center Stage

Great organizations do not just drive profits, they lead people, and they change the course of industries and sometimes our lives in the process. – **Start with Why**

Made in America

In 2008, one year prior to Reto making his decision to manufacture LEDs in our factory, the gentleman from MDL Transformers became ill. He called Reto and told him he had cancer. Reto knew he was dying. He looked at me and said that we needed to start making our own transformer or we were going to be "screwed." The owner's sons would inherit his company, MDL, and Reto knew after that phone call we would begin manufacturing our own version of that MDL transformer. We had sold a gazillion of them and needed to replace the transformer with one that was its equal or better.

We needed to become vertically integrated by designing, engineering, and manufacturing our own products in America. We brought in a mechanical and an electrical engineer.

We knocked it out of the ballpark and today we have better transformer made specifically for LED lighting systems. Our transformers are 1838 UL listed, have a lifetime warranty, and a failure rate of less than .0001 percent, which means 1 in 1,000. The LED transformers have a surge protection on the primary and the secondary. They are multi-tapped toroidal and guarantee that the system will run for a lifetime.

The market abandoned halogen lights. The integrated LED technology was where it was at and still is. In 2009, our partnership factory in Taiwan and of course all the factories in China were selling LED. The stuff was of very low quality, variable light, and failing almost immediately in the field due to a combination of heat hitting the chip and destroying it and the moisture in the air. It was like something out of a cracker jack box. ZERO innovation and quality sourcing or control. With us building our loyal following, we knew we could not sell a product that was guaranteed to fail in just a few months. We'd be out of business in a year, so we started making LED light fixtures and we could proudly say "Made in the USA."

All the innovation came from our WHY. We needed to make a high-quality product our dealers could stake their reputations on. We allowed our customers to collaborate, provide input, and express their needs on what we would build because they were out there in the trenches.

It was an uphill battle with Reto and the engineers working to analyze glues, temperatures, surges and efficiencies. Reto pushed and when the products would fail, we would push harder. The engineers were taxed with the challenges and Reto did not let up. Long hours, long days and nights of working with the guys. Trials and failures were learning lessons and there was a lot of frustration in the ranks, but everyone trusted Reto and knew that we would get there eventually.

This is what I love about our company. We are the American dream. American ingenuity mixed with hard work, perseverance and the abject belief that "it can happen" if you simply do the work. What is it they say? If you do almost anything for 10,000 hours, you become an expert at it? It felt like we were putting in the 10,000 hours. It was the most difficult thing to bring high-quality LED technology into the world that would stand the test of time and temperatures. LEDs are more sensitive than our cell phones. Heat and humidity are deadly to the LED's. Most manufacturers still haven't figured it out. And at first, we didn't either.

Before LED lighting came on the scene we sold tons of transformers and we were able to offer them at a low cost, which got the attention of the installers. Now we had our own improved transformer to sell and no worries because we made them ourselves in the good old USA.

As for fixtures, we had sold over 1 million of the F-7150's and F-777 spotlights, all halogen products.

"Can we talk to you about customer experience? We believe in the lighting demo and offering three quotes: good, better, best." I would get on the phone and sell, sell, sell.

That's how we built the business. We would teach people how to effectively use the lighting demo. NO ONE wanted to do it. It was at night and that meant giving up evening hours and they didn't see the value in it. But the demo... that's the sweet spot. When you can light the persons property and show them what they're getting when they buy, you have the sale. Here you have a black blank slate. When you turn the lights on, the customer doesn't want you to leave the property. But we have a whole chapter on that for you later in the book.

But we had been like everyone else; resellers. Not anymore. It was Reto who made the decision that it was time to bring manufacturing back to the U.S. and for Garden Light LED to control its own supply chain. He was the visionary on this and I needed to be his support system.

What and How

By 2009 we had built an amazing following. A percentage of our installers, at least twenty percent of them, were true Garden Light people. They were far more than clients. They'd come in to the office, go to our house; they were our friends.

Most people were using maybe 20 lights in the lighting design for a house. We were using 150. There's no sense in disappointing the customer who built a million-dollar house. That person is looking for ambiance, safety, even glamor. They want to create a sanctuary for themselves and their loved ones. These people work long hours and their home is their respite from the weary world. If you're going to light it; light it well.

Businesses wanted LED lighting as well. It was a game changer and the businesses that bought into using our lighting stood out against the competition. We learned more and more about color and how it effects mood and how to use it to reflect the places we lit. We'll talk a lot about that in another chapter; exciting and important stuff. Doing a demo for these folks is very impactful.

We became Garden Light LED. We did a complete reorganization of the company. We had our awesome transformer and then we made thousands of fixtures, sold them to our installers, and, guess what.

Our lights were failing.

We would field calls at all hours of the night. Our installers were freaking out and a lot of them were in that twenty percent - people that we were close to, who put their faith in us, and their businesses were on the line. We doubled down with our engineers and our suppliers.

What do we do?

How do we handle this hybrid technology?

The answer was to do whatever you have to do to fix it and fix it fast. We put millions of dollars into perfecting our product line.

Our installers were instrumental to our success. We were able to make product improvements rapidly due to our closeness with them. They were our boots on the ground and they knew what was wrong with the products, so we had accurate insight to help us move quickly and precisely. They provided us the ultimate testing ground.

Selecting LED Products

So, how do you select the LED products? Why should you choose to work with us?

Outdoor lighting has been around for decades. The evolution of outdoor lighting has advanced faster in this decade than any other. New technologies are in demand for many reasons, some of which include efficacy, sustainability, energy consumption, consumer demand, and quality of light. With new technologies entering the world rapidly, LED has provided the lighting industry both new and old opportunities in this space. LED lighting professionals are desirable, and a necessary commodity and they have a hundred different sources to choose from. As I mentioned, one of the main problems LED lighting professionals are faced with is that they do not have a direct relationship with their supplier, which means the manufacturer only cares about them when they are purchasing products. Secondly, they do not love the products they represent. Because, while they may look beautiful on the outside, they know that the products are made with subpar materials that will corrode over time. Knowing this upfront, they are forced to lower their prices in hopes of mitigating problems that lie ahead; it rarely does. In addition, they often feel isolated and alone as business owners.

We changed that for our installers. We created American made products they could trust at prices that allowed them to compete and make a very good profit on. In addition, we offered them something most companies don't, full support.

We're here for our installers in every capacity, not just with great products and service, but with high-quality marketing materials that they can bring with them to presentations, a lighting demo kit that lets them set up a kick-ass demo in less than 15 minutes and now a full service digital marketing department that does all the heavy lifting for them in their target market area. Our installers are our real why. We're smart enough to know that building up their businesses means success for all of us.

The People You Meet

The lighting industry is a people business. It is a positive experience and enhances the lives of the people you serve. I find this is one of the greatest benefits of the business. The reward and sense of accomplishment is a continuous theme when helping American entrepreneurs grow a thriving business.

The reward in being a LED lighting solution and service provider is extremely fulfilling. But, you must be flexible and do a lot to provide your clients an excellent experience through and through. I'm not saying run around without order, I am saying the exact opposite. In most cases, lighting professionals don't give themselves credit, they do not think of themselves as entrepreneurial leaders in the community. I promise you if you position yourself as an American entrepreneur, you will be a leader.

We've all have heard the age-old adage; timing is everything. Being at the right place at the right time is essential to a company offering a product and selling a service. You are at the right place and the time is now. Goldman Saks ranks LED as the fasting growing segment and recommends that investments be made in LED technology today. Digital marketing is becoming the norm and, in as little as five years, will be the only way to be sustainable and ready for the future. Adoption can be slow in the beginning because the lighting industry as a whole has never thought in these terms unless it's a franchise model; frankly, the franchise model is not even there. You must be strategically working a plan that includes bettering yourself, becoming the best lighting professional in the market, having a standard of excellence for yourself, your employees and your customers.

Because this takes time and getting out of your comfort zone, not everyone is on the bandwagon.

Once we got our mojo working we were unstoppable. But just selling the best American-made lighting products on the market wasn't enough. We realized something was missing. The world was changing; technology was changing, and we had to change with it. We began to recognize what the rest of the world was embracing. Digital marketing.

We put together a professional and highly-skilled marketing team. We needed to add web design, social media management, content writing, and graphic arts to our list of skills, so we hired people to take those seats on the bus. This time, I was Walt and Reto was my Roy. I was the visionary and Reto backed me 100% with funding and support in everything from hiring staff and sitting through meeting after meeting to constant encouragement.

We went to our installers and pitched the idea and invited them to our first congress, early in 2015. All of the eggs in our basket are with our contractors. We needed them to understand our vision and get on board with our strategy to make them far more successful.

We doubled down with them too. Along with our new team, we came up with a comprehensive digital marketing platform that gives eligible partners, people who are established and meet the requirements, a cutting-edge way to market themselves. We call it our Master Dealer Program.

Let me tell you a little bit about our Master Dealer Program:

Once an installer signs on, we appoint them the designated market representative in their area. We provide them a co-marketed website. In essence, they get a marketing agency at no cost. We provide the website. We get their listings on review sites and get them five-star reviews. We blog for them, write content, create their gallery of photos and do all of their social media posting. They have top quality, full-color brochures of the products to take with them on presentations. This kind of marketing is expensive and invaluable. Companies pay a fortune to have a marketing firm do for them what we do for our Master Dealers, but it's worth it.

Before that can happen, the first requirement is that they must attend our dealer congress. At these events, we bring entrepreneurial moguls to work with our team. It's a 48-hour, intensive training boot camp and we tell them, "strap on your seatbelt."

The cost to attend is $2,000 and they leave with at least $2,000 worth of product, specifically every company gets one of our demo kits that include our top products in a hard, black rolling case valued at $1999. With that kit, you can roll up onto a client's property and have a complete lighting demo live for them to view in roughly 10 – 15 minutes. We record the sessions and use them for future training videos so we're always forward thinking. Participants get both video and audio recordings of our keynote speakers to take with them for inspiration.

Their hotel stay, meals, training manual and certificate of completion are all included in the cost, so it's well worth the price. Once they complete the seminar, they're eligible to participate in the Master Dealer Program. If they don't understand what this can do for them after those 48-hours and the training we provide, then they aren't a good fit.

We had 60 of our best installers show up the first year in 2015. The second year we nearly doubled that with over 80 in attendance and this February, we are expecting 120 attendees.

So, what are some of the qualities you should possess to be a good fit for our Master Dealer Program?

You have to have passion.

You have to want to succeed.

You need to be willing to do the work.

You have to be willing to create strategic partnerships with people like us.

You must embrace the entrepreneurial spirit.

You must educate yourself.

You must embrace the concept of digital marketing.

52% of the Fortune 500 companies have disappeared. That's telling. We teach the value of being relationship-centric, how to attract the right customers, ones that are fun and profitable to work with, how to gain, keep, and receive referrals from customers and how digital marketing can help you become the most highly-paid, highly-valued LED lighting professional in your local market.

We want our contractors to do whatever they can to be more rooted and professional through continuing education. It's all about credibility. Our Master Dealer Program provides that education and lends to that credibility. We don't want you to go the way of the dinosaur and we know that the best way to increase business in today's changing world is to embrace the technology that's available.

> Truth is, I'm not happy with the status quo. I want to build American entrepreneurs and that's just what we're doing.

Owning your local digital landscape costs time, money and takes a lot of patience. The good news is if you embrace localized digital marketing today, you can be certain that your competition won't, and you will be in position as the authority and go-to lighting solution. Remember I said it takes time and patience. By the time your competition makes the move, it will be too late. It takes foresight and commitment to this strategy, and if you act now and begin the arduous process, the space will be yours and your company will own it!

Businesses, both large and small, are implementing these best practice strategies.

There are four things you must commit your life to today:

1. Using great American made products

2. Delivering the intangible - undisputed service

3. Having a comprehensive digital marketing strategy and execution

4. Creating an uncontested customer experience

Businesses need to proactively ask their customers to post a review to Google, Yelp or other business directories where they have an established account. They can offer deals or discounts for additional services as thanks for posting a review. However, it should not be interpreted as a bribe – it should be seen as an incentive. Providing an exceptional customer experience and then asking at the right time is critical.

I met a gentleman 10 years ago and made the undeniable mistake of not taking heed to what he was prophesizing then. His name was John V. Rizzo. He and Michael Santoro wrote a book together called Niche Dominance. He called my company out of the blue and set an appointment to come in. This conversation and strategy was new to me, I was interested, however did not do anything about it. I didn't see it coming, but I sure get it now.

These two gentlemen were pioneers in the space and had knowledge that has been captured by all successful and prominent companies today.

More good news is that a drone cannot deliver service. If you commit to partnering and adopting cutting-edge digital marketing strategies, you will own a successful company for many years to come.

Reto and I have learned a lot working together. We've been through some hard times, but we persevered. We had a pretty short courtship after all, and in reality, we got to know each other deeply only after our first child was born. Business was the glue that helped us stick together and follow through for our kids, our company, our employees and our customers. We do what we do because we truly believe that lights make life better for the people we serve. We realize that customers buy lighting when they can see it. You take an existing dark space and light it up, and you've got a customer. Everything we sell is low voltage landscape lighting. We can pop up a 50-light demo in 10 - 15 minutes. No one can do that.

Truth is, I'm not happy with the status quo. I want to build American entrepreneurs and that's just what we're doing. Steve Jobs wouldn't let up. He wanted to make that dent in the universe and so do I. Jobs was the king of emerging innovation. We are doing the same thing. Our engineers are constantly working on new products and helping push the technology forward.

That what excites me.

I love that we're agile. We listen to our contractors and give them what they need, even if we have to create it ourselves. That's what makes us special.

And we get to provide jobs for people. Like Henry Ford, we create jobs right here in America.

No one in our industry has had the courage to embrace digital marketing.

No one but us.

Chapter 3

Dare
to Be Different

Many people buy franchises. It sounds simple. Everything is planned out for you and, if you follow the pattern and do what's expected of you, you should succeed. Right?

You don't have to buy a Franchise to make a Fortune

Did you know that Henry Ford played a part in the actual design of the franchise model? Once he was able to get mass production down to a science, he knew, like Singer and his sewing machines, that he had to hone in on the distribution side of the business too. He did so by creating a franchise (dealer) network all across the country.

We don't typically think of car dealerships as franchises, but they are.

"The two most important requirements for major success are: first, being in the right place at the right time, and second, doing something about it."

Any guess whose quote that is? Maybe this will help you figure it out. He also said this:

"We take the hamburger business more seriously than anyone else."

Both of those quotes are from Ray Kroc, the founder of the franchise to end all franchises, McDonald's. Talk about being in the right place at the right time; and you have to admit, he did something about it. He took hamburgers, fries, and milkshakes seriously and many, many people bought into that franchise model.

There's no variation on the theme though. No "doing your own thing." You can walk into a McDonalds in Tampa, Florida or Madison, Wisconsin and unless you look out the window, nothing would look different. Everything, down to the ketchup packets will be the same.

Modern day franchises provide simple entrepreneurial solutions for people that want to own their own business. Franchising has been around for hundreds of years. The franchise model offers a potential business owner the possibility of success based on a concept, solution, product or service that someone else has created for them. Theoretically, you're paying for the idea; a one-stop shop, a business in a box. People like the franchising business concept because they believe if a business represents a successful model, they can create success just the way the franchise creator had.

Business by rote; like paint by numbers.

But there are "The Rules."

You must follow the franchisors' rules. There's really no wiggle room here.

Franchise systems need rules. They need a lot of them. They're there to keep things uniform. Rules are not put in place to aggravate you.

Let's look at the advantages to franchising

Buying a franchise can be a quick way to set up your own business without starting from scratch. But there are also a number of drawbacks.

The good stuff:

- Franchising reduces the risk of business failure. Your business is based on a proven idea. You can check how successful other franchises are before committing yourself.

- Products and services will have already established a market share. Therefore, there will be no need for market testing.

- You can use a recognized brand name and trademark. You benefit from any advertising or promotion by the owner of the franchise - the 'franchisor'.

- The franchisor gives you support - usually as a complete package including training, help setting up the business, a manual telling you how to run the business and ongoing advice.

- No prior experience is needed, as the training received from the franchisor should ensure that the franchisee establishes the skills required to operate the franchise.

- A franchise enables a small business to compete with big businesses, more so than an independent small business, due to the pool of support from the franchisor and network of other franchisees.

- You usually have exclusive rights in your territory. The franchisor won't sell any other franchises in the same territory.

- Financing the business may be easier. Banks are sometimes more likely to lend money to buy a franchise with a good reputation.

- You can benefit from communicating and sharing ideas with, and receiving support from, other franchisees in the network.

- Relationships with suppliers have already been established.

So, why shouldn't you buy a Franchise?

Franchising isn't perfect. That's because humans are involved.

Disadvantages of franchising.
Some legitimate concerns:

- Costs may be higher than you expect. As well as the initial costs of buying the franchise, you pay continuing management service fees and you may have to agree to buy products from the franchisor.

- The franchise agreement usually includes restrictions on how you can run the business. You might not be able to make changes to suit your local market.

- You may find that after time, ongoing franchisor monitoring becomes intrusive.

- The franchisor might go out of business.

- Other franchisees could give the brand a bad reputation.

- You may find it difficult to sell your franchise - you can only sell it to someone approved by the franchisor.

- All profits (a percentage of sales) are usually shared with the franchisor.

- The inflexible nature of a franchise may restrict your ability to introduce changes to the business to respond to the market or make the business grow.

Franchise Fee

You'll be required to pay a franchise fee up-front. This one-time investment *(per franchise unit)* is the cost of entry. It's the licensing fee. The franchise fee allows you to use all the franchisors proprietary information legally. The franchise fee is normally around $30,000-$50,000 on average. It could be a bit less, and it could be a bit more. But, it's there and it's a required payment. That's a lot of money.

Royalties

As a franchisee, you'll be paying the franchisor a percentage of your gross sales each and every month you're a franchisee. Percentages vary. I've seen food franchise royalties that are 5% and royalties for **consulting types of franchises** that are as high as 12% of sales.

In a society of instant gratification, technology has created the idea that you have to have everything right now.

Let's say your franchise sales are $25,000 per month. If the royalty is 5%, that means the franchisor will collect a check from you for $1250.00. That's $15,000 a year that goes to the franchisor. Now, double it. If your franchise is doing $50,000 a month in sales, you're sending in a $2,500 check each month. That's $30,000 a year!

For the most part, you're required to purchase your products and supplies from your franchisor.

If you're a Dairy Queen franchisee, you'll be purchasing your ice cream from Dairy Queen headquarters-*as it should be.* In the past, some franchisees have banded together to try to change that requirement in order to save some money. Some have even won out and *have* been able to purchase things from non-franchisor suppliers. But, don't count on that happening in the franchise system you're a part of.

In most cases, you'll be paying a percentage of your gross sales *(in addition to the royalties)* to the franchisor. Figure 1%-2%. It's a small number, but it *does* add up.

As a matter of fact, it *really* adds up-at least psychologically if the franchisors' marketing is average at best. It's no fun paying into a marketing plan you have little or no say in.

Find out ahead of time…way before you sign your franchise agreement and send in the franchise fee, just how good their marketing is. Talk to a dozen or so existing franchisees. Ask them straight-out if they're getting a good return on their marketing investment. Don't Buy a Franchise Unless You Know What You're Doing!

So, owning a franchise lets you be part of a system that could work. But if you're not the type of person that wants to be part of a machine, how do you differentiate yourself from other business professionals in your field and still succeed?

Blue Ocean Strategy

I'm a big fan of something called Blue Ocean Strategy.

Blue Ocean Strategy is a marketing theory from a book published in 2005 which was written by **W. Chan Kim** and Renée Mauborgne. Based on a study of 150 strategic moves spanning more than a hundred years and thirty industries, Kim & Mauborgne argue that companies can succeed by creating «blue oceans» of uncontested market space, as opposed to «red oceans» where competitors fight for dominance, the analogy being that an ocean full of vicious competition turns red with blood.

In the book the authors correlate success stories across industries and the formulation of strategies that create unconventional success – a strategy termed as "blue ocean strategy". Unlike the "red ocean strategy", the conventional approach to business of beating competition, the "blue ocean strategy" tries to align innovation with utility, price and cost positions. The red ocean concept suggests that consumers make their choices based on product/service differentiation and lower cost. Blue ocean strategy suggests that both differentiation and lower costs are achievable simultaneously.

The right strategic move can create a "blue ocean" for any business. The book examines the experience of companies in areas as diverse as watches, wine, cement, computers, automobiles, textiles, coffee makers, airlines, retailers, even the circus and builds upon the idea of "value innovation" being the cornerstone of a blue ocean strategy. Value innovation is the alignment of innovation with utility, price and cost positions. This creates an uncontested market space and makes competition irrelevant.

Red oceans represent most of the industries in existence today – the known market space. In the red oceans, the boundaries are defined and accepted, and the competitive rules of the game are known. Companies try to outperform their rivals to grab a greater share of product or service demand. As the market space gets crowded, prospects for profits and growth are reduced. Products become commodities or niche, and cutthroat competition turns the ocean bloody, hence the term "red oceans".

Blue oceans, in contrast, denote all the industries not in existence today – the unknown market space, untainted by competition. In blue oceans, demand is *created* rather than fought over. There is ample opportunity for growth that is both profitable and rapid. In blue oceans, competition is irrelevant because the rules of the game are waiting to be set. Blue ocean is an analogy to describe the wider, deeper potential of market space that is not yet explored.

So, how do you apply Blue Ocean Strategy and Own a "Million Dollar LED Lighting Business?"

The answer: Be an Innovative and Digitally Dominant Business.

"Whatever the mind of man can conceive and believe it can achieve."

- Napoleon Hill, Think and Grow Rich

Digital marketing – the big game changer

In a society of instant gratification, technology has created the idea that you have to have everything right now.

Most of the people working in our industry are still mucking about in the bloody waters of the red ocean. They market themselves using traditional marketing, but so does the competition.

What constitutes traditional marketing:

- **Ads in local publications** – often very expensive to run

- **Coupons** - or special offers in flyers, direct mail pieces, or magazines – often thrown out or never opened

- **Networking** – joining groups, chambers of commerce – time consuming and limited in the number of people you reach. These can also become costly to join and keep up with.

- **Door hangers and flyers** – printing costs, delivery methods can also be expensive and again, more often than not, tossed out. However, these can be very effective if allowed. Many communities, especially in the target market areas for high-end properties that will be seeking outdoor lighting, won't allow for this kind of marketing.

- **Radio or TV ads** – very, very, costly, though often effective.

- **Websites** – These are a must in both traditional and digital marketing. A good website is worth its weight in gold, but it must be keyword rich, responsive so that it sizes for phones and tablets and be maintained. A stagnant website is like a runner on a track. He's in the race, but barely moving if at all. Websites that are active, include blogs, refresh content often, and are attached to social media are running full-speed ahead on the track. That's where digital marketing comes in.

These are all very effective ways to get the word out about your lighting design business and people using traditional marketing are certainly getting work, but so is the competition. By using traditional marketing there are really only two ways to win over the customer and get the sale.

1. You offer better service and products
2. You're cheaper

Price is almost always the key factor when you're in the red ocean model of doing business. If you've been in business a while and have a good reputation in your local market, that surely helps with credibility. But the guy that beats you for the job may also have a good reputation and then price becomes the main issue.

Digital Marketing

The best way to move out of the red ocean and into the clear, cool waters of the blue ocean is to embrace digital marketing. There are many industries that have realized the value in making use of the technology that today's buyers, particularly the millennials, are engrossed in. Savvy realtors, restaurants, and many service industries are coming on board and moving away from traditional marketing.

If they can't find you in seconds on their phone, they don't find you at all.

What are some of the key components of digital marketing

- **Blogging** – adding keyword driven articles that position you as an expert in the field will put you at the head of the class and move your listing on Google and other search engines to the top of the pile and out of the red ocean into the blue.

- **Social Media** – yes, you're sick of hearing it but you have to have a strong presence on platforms like Facebook, Twitter, Instagram and Pinterest. Your potential clients are there, and they will be looking for you. Integrating that with a well-maintained website will create buzz and excitement about your business.

- **Online Reviews** – Getting everyone you install a lighting system for to review you is literally money in the bank. Today, everyone looks at reviews. This is something that has to be cultivated and monitored. Bad reviews can kill a company. The crazy guys at South Park did an entire episode devoted to the power of YELP and the people who are crazy Yelpers. It was called "You're not Yelping" because people look at those reviews. If they're bad, they don't go to that restaurant, salon, or auto mechanic. Caveat Emptor, let the buyer beware. But if they're good, they chose that business over the others.

- **Websites** – Yup, this falls into both categories as I said earlier. But you need to have a good website, not one that your cousin built in 2002 that doesn't size to fit on a phone. Your site has to be easy to navigate, have great images, easy ways to contact you with the flick of a thumb. That's how people buy things today.

If you want to dominate your local market, you must be the easiest business to find and contact. You need to be the "Guru," the expert that they find when they see articles written by you. You need blog posts that tell them what kind of lighting fixtures to avoid, which ones will need replacing in two years, and which ones to go with; the ones that have lifetime guarantees. Be the go to guy for all their questions, the one with the great Google and Yelp reviews whose company name keeps popping up in their social media feed, and price will be far less important.

People who buy houses that cost in excess of one million dollars aren't as concerned about a slightly lower cost nearly as much as they are about *value.*

Be the company that everyone values. Be the company that is VALUABLE because you are everywhere, and you know everything about lighting design, great lighting products, great installation, and customer service.

That's how you win in today's market. That's how you dominate the local market and create a clear blue ocean because, frankly, the other guys aren't doing it. The lighting design community has not embraced digital marketing overall, but Garden Light LED has.

When you work with us as a Master Dealer, we do all your digital marketing for you. We have a team of web designers, social media experts, content and blog writers who handle all of that for you. It's like having your own personal marketing team on your staff. Hiring a staff like ours is a very expensive proposition, but you don't have to do that. You just have to qualify to be a Master Dealer and our team becomes your team.

The one other thing that will turn your ocean blue is our unique lighting demo kit. None of your competitors can do a lighting demo like ours and we will teach you how and give you the tools you need to do the best lighting demo in the business.

Yes, it's a process and you have to learn new things. Education can take time and effort, but it's worth it if you want to take your business to the next level and compete in the modern landscape.

Success is hard. Failure is easy. Don't fear becoming a millionaire. You already know how to light a million-dollar home.

Chapter 4

US Manufacturing vs. Global Instability

Find a US Manufacturer

American Innovation -
American made LED technology

Made in the U.S.A. is hot again and so is the number of manufacturing jobs that are returning to the U.S. or coming to the U.S for the first time. The United States of America is, and always has been, a global economic superpower. Once again, customers are clamoring for the latest Land of Liberty made products. Something made overseas does not possess the character or qualities a true American entrepreneur or American-made product does.

Last December, the president said, "We want to create and sell products all over the world that are stamped with three simple words 'Made in America.' That's our goal."

It's our goal too, our biggest goal, in fact; that and creating jobs here in America and building up the businesses that work with us, buy our products, and become part of our Master Dealer family.

Manufacturing is the highest multiplier effect of any economic sector. American manufacturing functions as the nation's economic engine, it creates economic growth and is crucial for all developed economies.

What sets manufacturing apart from the many other sectors of the economy is the commitment to continuing training and education. When you manufacture products the way we do, you get to see your impact daily. When we make a new lighting fixture, we get to hold it in our hands, test it and make sure it's perfect before we send it out to our installers.

It's a good feeling to hold something that you made; the weight of it in your hands is so compelling, so powerful.

"This is ours. We made this and it's great."

And we get to provide opportunities for people to raise their average income and living standards. It's the most important cause of economic growth. We add to that growth, not just in our facility, but with our installers and now with our Master Dealers. When you become a Master Dealer, you get to be part of the fabric that makes up American entrepreneurship.

Some facts about American manufacturing:

- Manufacturers contributed $2.17 trillion to the U.S. economy.
- There were 256,363 firms in the manufacturing sector.

- There are 12.33 million manufacturing workers in the United States, accounting for 9 percent of the workforce.

- Manufacturing supports 18.5 million jobs in the United States.

- 3.5 million manufacturing jobs will be needed over the next decade.

- Over the past 25 years, U.S.-manufactured goods exports more than quadrupled, it reached an all-time high, for the fifth consecutive year, over $1.403 trillion.

- Manufacturing in the United States would be the ninth-largest economy in the world.

- Manufacturers in the United States perform more than three-quarters of all private-sector research and development (R&D) in the nation, driving more innovation than any other sector.

Science, technology, and industry have not only profoundly shaped America's economic success, but have also contributed to its distinct political institutions, social structure, educational system and cultural identity. American values of limited government, meritocracy, entrepreneurship, and self-sufficiency are drawn from its legacy of pioneering technical advances.

We get to be part of that and so do you.

This is how America won WW2 and many wars before that. We rapidly manufactured and automated planes and tanks and turned metal here in the USA. We dominated global manufacturing for years.

It was part of my roots, the auto industry in America, that manufactured the tanks, trucks, jeeps and airplanes retooling factories to make all of that as well as bombs, torpedoes, steel helmets and ammunition. At the beginning of the war, the British and French placed large orders for aircraft with American manufacturers and the US Congress approved plans to increase its air force by 3,000 planes. In May 1940, Franklin D. Roosevelt called for the production of 185,000 airplanes, 120,000 tanks, 55,000 anti-aircraft guns and 18 million tons of merchant shipping to be manufactured in two years. Adolf Hitler was told by his advisors that this was American propaganda. Not surprising that they wouldn't believe we could do so, considering that in 1939, annual aircraft production for the US military was less than 3,000 planes. But by the end of the war, US factories had produced 300,000 planes, and by 1944 America had produced two-thirds of the Allied military equipment used in the war. Talk about American ingenuity, pride and manufacturing prowess.

Challenges

Over the 21-year lifespan of Garden Light LED, we've found that there are three main challenges that most LED lighting professionals face in their business.

First, selecting the right manufacturer is extremely important and I'll tell you why. Hundreds of lighting professionals/entrepreneurs have told me they do not have a direct relationship with the manufacturer of their products, which means the supplier doesn't have a vested interest in their success and only cares about them when they are purchasing product.

Second, they don't really love the products they represent. While many may look good on the outside, they realize in most cases, the products are made with subpar quality materials. This will eventually upset their customers down the road, due to breakage and instability. Knowing this upfront, they end up offering discounts in hopes that this will minimize the troubles that lie ahead.

It rarely does.

And it's embarrassing. The key to a truly successful business is reputation. Referrals are the name of the game. Who's going to refer a company that sold them inferior products that break easily and quickly?

Third, they are alone as business owners with very little support; they feel isolated because they have to go it alone. Garden Light LED solves these problems by having a vested interest in the business of our installers. Our reps aren't customers, they are partners. When they succeed, we succeed. The big advantage our partners have is that Garden Light LED's unprecedented quality manufacturing gives them a product they can stand behind. Therefore, they don't feel pressured into lowering their costs, which means our dealers have a higher margin of profit.

Our business building tools, combined with our proprietary training, gives our dealers the support they need and has proven to double our partners business in 2-3 years. Our research shows that no other LED lighting manufacturer offers this one-to-one business strategy. And then, of course, there's our Master Dealer Program.

The reason I'm so passionate about this is because I personally developed this program, so I know how life changing it can be. Manufacturing is in my blood. As I told you, I grew up fast on the streets of East Detroit, and I was often reminded of the legends of the past. Dedicated factory workers who made an honest living working for companies like Ford, General Motors, and Chrysler surrounded me. Factory workers like my father, an engineer in these factories, and my uncle, an executive who left my aunt a plentiful retirement when he died. Bringing ingenuity into the world and working with entrepreneurs, allows me to feel close to what I've always known. My husband Reto and I made a decision to dedicate our lives to our great American dream and to bring as many business owners as we could with us along the way. We are known as the business that builds other businesses, that helps others live their American dream.

While many other lighting manufacturers offer 3- to 5-year warranties, all of Garden Light LED products come with an unheard of 20-year warranty. Our dealers love boasting about that. Of the 500 dealers Garden Light LED have throughout North America, thirty have generated multi-million-dollar companies.

Whatever lighting fixtures you choose to use it's very important that they are tested and approved. All Garden Light LED products are rigorously tested, not only by us, but are tested and certified by Electronic Testing Laboratories (ETL) Interek and Underwriters Laboratory Certification (UL).

Who they are:

ETL Interek

The Electronic Testing Laboratories (ETL) Listed Mark is proof that the product has been independently tested and meets the applicable published standard for compliance to North American safety standards. Authorities having Jurisdiction (AHJ's) and code officials across the US and Canada accept the ETL Listed Mark as proof of product compliance to published industry standards. Every day, more and more consumers recognize it on products they purchase as a symbol of safety. It's the fastest growing safety certification in North America and is featured on millions of products sold by major retailers and distributors every day, formally confirming that your products and services meet all trusted external and internal standards. As global markets grow and expand, there are more consumers seeking safe, reliable, and, increasingly, eco-conscious products. Seeing the ETL Interek approval on products means peace of mind. It's something you can show clients and it gives you more confidence when using ETL Interek certified safe products.

The key to a truly successful business is reputation.

UL

UL stands for Underwriters Laboratory Certification (UL) and they have been around for over 100 years. The company is a world leader in product safety testing and certification. UL works with customers and stakeholders to help them navigate market complexity. UL certifies the responsible design, production, marketing and purchase of goods so that you know you are selling safer, more secure, more sustainable products that are specifically made for outdoors and wet locations.

Global Instability – why you should buy American made products

How does political instability impact Global Sourcing?

Political instability is an enormous threat to the success of companies operating in the global supply chain arena. Organizations with global sourcing needs must understand the potential negative impact that political instability can have on productivity, quality and relationships and create strategies to mitigate risk.

Political instability represents bottom line threats to global supply chains.

Some facts to be aware of:

- Eastern Europe and Southeast Asia are two areas where global sourcing is expected to expand the most.

- Political risks have increased dramatically since 2014 in the BRICS countries (Brazil, Russia, India, China and South Africa).

- Countries with weak political stability are more likely to experience decision-making by government officials that negatively impacts businesses.

Political Instability and the Impact on Global Supply Chains

Political instability is the propensity for regime or government change, political upheaval, violence, instability and uncertainty in government policy, such as regulatory, tax, property, or human rights law. Any political shift involving one or more of these issues has the potential to cause concern at a local level as well as create major global supply chain turmoil.

So basically, buying from China might not be as stable as you'd like.

These shifts could result in delivery delays and re-routed resources when political unrest occurs. Organizations and businesses must proactively prepare for adverse conditions around the world.

The world is in a fair bit of political turmoil. This is why we chose to spend the time and money to invest in ourselves and build our products in our own factory in the USA using American workers and American ingenuity. We didn't want to rely on materials coming from places that were suffering from political unrest and take the chance that we would be waiting on supplies from those places to fill orders and keep our partners waiting. We didn't want to chance getting inferior products and have no recourse when the suppliers were unable to make good on their promises.

Manufacturing here in the US gave us the opportunity to hire people; to give them the chance to build new and exciting things. It's impactful seeing that.

What makes manufacturing so exciting is the chance to create and make things and that means lots of new and different jobs are created as well. We hire curious, imaginative thinkers who are willing to look at things from new perspectives. They consider the "what if' and "why not."

Our engineers are creative problem solvers with a lot of experience in the field. We love new technology such as 3-D printing and computer-aided design and we are looking forward to the innovation that will come over the next 20 or so years.

We're excited to be part of all of that.

Garden Light LED has established a respected legacy brand. We want our dealers to own their own legacy brand too. The society we live in today demands instant gratification, wants everything now rather than working hard for future generations. In a world of rapid consumption, values can be lost. We live in a time when very few people are willing to sacrifice today for tomorrow. With a poor emphasis on self-knowledge and core values, giving up has become the norm unlike the generations before us who paved the way for our future success. It's a "What's in it for me, right here, right now." world.

That attitude won't get you far though. If you want to be an American entrepreneur, you have to be willing to grow, learn and change for the better. Then you will be on track to own an exceptional lighting company that is known for its character, quality and service. You can build a business that saves money, that lives below its means, is wise and nimble. You can build a business that builds businesses for future generations, showing respect for mankind and our planet, with the understanding of the personal role you can have in supporting the American economy.

Garden Light LED is and has been, since inception, debt free and privately held. We owe zero dollars and we are owed zero dollars. Everything that comes in and leaves the door is paid in full. This goes back to 1996 when Reto lost everything. He learned this principle because of the mistakes he made in the past. Garden Light LED inventories over two million dollars-worth of finished LED goods and one million dollars in bill of materials.

Why? Because Reto likes to have six months of inventory ready for our partners should any situation arise. We stock 3,000k, but all fixtures are available in 2,700k, 2,800k and 5,000k.

We're the boy scouts of the LED lighting fixture world. We're always prepared. You don't have to worry about problems overseas or international shipping issues. We have a warehouse filled with the goods you need.

We've built the better mousetrap, one that's made in the USA. But that's only part of what makes us successful. Embracing the future with digital marketing and continually educating our installer partners so they can grow their business is the rest of the puzzle. We don't just want to sell lighting fixtures, we want to build a lighting empire. Our installers are the key to that and our Master Dealer program is the final puzzle piece.

So, how can you become part of our family? How can you apply your American spirit and become a highly successful lighting professional? We believe the answer lies with our Master Dealer program.

What does being in the Master Dealer program entail?

Garden Light LED has been working on our digital marketing platform for almost two years. It is not a commitment that we take lightly. We have put significant time and money into developing these tools to effectively grow the businesses of our Master Dealers. It is only through the growth of our dealers that Garden Light LED will be able to grow its business and create more jobs right here in the USA. Therefore, all our marketing initiatives, business development efforts and technology acquisitions completely focus on growing the sales volume and market share of our dealers. This is how Garden Light LED has been successful since its inception and how it will be successful in the future.

A Summary Explanation of the Digital Marketing Platform

The digital marketing platform is a grouping of 5 very powerful tools designed to help our family of dealers significantly grow their business in their local markets.

1. **Online Reputation** – We seek good client reviews and address bad ones quickly.

2. **Social Media** – Posting across platforms keeps you fresh in the minds of your target market.

3. **Search Engine Optimization** – Being found in searches is the ultimate goal and it's a science.

4. **Directory Listings** – You must be listed EVERYWHERE!

5. **Customer Relationship Management (CRM)** – We are customer-centric, make them happy and they will refer you to EVERYONE.

Garden Light LED has introduced a revolutionary marketing solution for the outdoor LED lighting industry that will change the way our family of dealers grows their businesses.

The Master Dealer Partnership Includes:

- Co-Marketed responsive websites
- Online Reputation Management
- Social Media Channel Distribution
- Search Engine Optimization
- Business Directory Listings
- Customer Relationship Management
- Access to innovative fixture technology
- Integrated online ordering system
- Leadership workshops and events
- Installation Product training
- Marketing Promotion Services
- Special rates on demonstration cases
- Dealer Certification Certificate
- On-going recommendations and newsletters to stay ahead of the curve
- Specialized access to our engineers, warranty representatives and sales team

Some Master Dealer Benefits Include:

- Right to sell and install a very high quality and dependable LED product
- Product training certification
- Excellent technical and warranty support
- Specialized access to engineers for technical support
- Sophisticated branding and marketing materials
- Intelligent online order entry

- Logo merchandise store
- Special pricing bundles
- Product and specification sheet downloads
- Photometrics and IES reports
- Comprehensive business development and marketing support
- Formalized training and certification support
- Personalized co-marketed website
- Dealer Platform on-boarding and training
- Geo-targeted digital marketing
- Real-time lead generation and reporting
- Social presence and reputation management
- Online directory listing standardization

No, it's not a franchise and you don't pay franchise fees or have to be part of a cookie cutter business like a McDonalds, but there are some requirements for being part of the program.

Our ongoing Master Dealer Requirements Include:

- Complete the application
- Meet all eligibility requirements
- Comprehensive product and installation training
- Sign a Master Dealer Agreement
- Submit a 12-month rolling forecast
- Yearly Dealer Congress attendance
- Serve on a Master Dealer committee
- Respond to sales leads within one business day
- Comply with GLLED product presentation requirements

- Comply with GLLED product installation requirements

We're on the cutting edge with both our lighting technology, and with our digital marketing technology. We're not at the mercy of world politics and upheavals. We're paving the way for American entrepreneurs to become American millionaires in the lighting industry. Our Master Dealer program can do that for anyone that puts in the effort.

Chapter 5

Get Incorporated
and Get Going

From an article in CNN Money Magazine – January 2017
The vast Wells Fargo branch network is shrinking.
Wells Fargo announced plans on Friday to shut down more than 400 bank branches by the end of 2018. That's on top of the 84 locations it pulled the plug on in 2016.

From an article in PHILADELPHIA (CNN) - January 2018
Wells Fargo, scrambling to cut costs and offset soaring legal expenses, plans to pull the plug on 800 more bank branches by 2020.

From an article in USA Today January 2018
Sam's Club closing dozens of stores; some being converted to distribution centers 63 to be exact!

Why am I telling you about these business closings? What relevance does this have to LED Lighting?

America is literally one of the only countries in the world where someone can lose or quit their job one day and create a business doing whatever it is they love the next. And with hard work, commitment and determination, anyone could generate a successful business that they own.

We could just manufacture and sell lighting fixtures all day long. In fact, we do just that. But that's not where our passion lies. It lies with showing people how they can build a million-dollar lighting business and never worry again that they're being downsized or forced to stay in a dead-end job they hate.

When Reto was belly-up, living in his car, he got a line of credit from a friend for $2000. Ironically, that same amount is all a person would need to attend our Dealer Congress and get started with us. No big franchise fees, no expensive storefront to buildout, no strict set of rules that boxes you in to one way of doing things.

Some of the people that come to our Dealer Congress are already in the lighting business and some are in related businesses and want to add lighting to the services they offer. But some are potential American entrepreneurs who are ready to make a change, take a chance and build a reliable business. Those folks are our real success stories and we have plenty of them.

I want to tell you a story about our son's hockey coach Gary Parkhurst. Gary grew up in Pennsylvania and is married to his high-school sweetheart. They joke that he came from the rough part of town and she was an uptown girl. They have two boys together and moved to Florida after Gary got out of the military. Gary served four years in the army and is currently still employed with a government agency and is our son's hockey coach. Gary and Reto hung out at hockey games and practices and got to know one another pretty well. Gary learned about outdoor LED lighting in talking with Reto about our company and what we do. To Reto, this is very familiar. Gary's story was not unlike that of Kyle, a former Air Force firefighter that we mentored and helped start his own successful landscape lighting company, which now generates almost four million dollars annually. After some discussion, Gary decided to take the plunge and has now started his own lighting design company, working with us, starting exactly in the manner

Learn from others. Success leaves clues.

Kyle did. He went to our Dealer Congress and is part of our Master Dealer program. He is already selling lighting design packages and is loving his work. He's on track to create a million-dollar company and all because he became friendly with Reto, the father of one of the kids he coaches.

This business is great for exiting military personnel. They have the drive and the discipline to learn the skills needed. The military teaches men and women to work hard and be respectful of others. We can teach them everything else they need to know to make this business work for them and we love working with them; seeing someone that's served our country come home and build a great life for themselves and their families.

The funny thing is, now that everyone at hockey knows about Gary and what he's doing, lots of folks have approached us that want to own their own business too. These people, Kyle and Gary, were in the right place at the right time. Make no mistake, it's not easy. We showed them the opportunity. They did the hard work of taking the steps needed. After that, the real work of learning and training began, and they are the ones that showed the American entrepreneurial spirit and dedication to get it done.

What are the steps to getting started?

Get Incorporated

First, you need to create a business name.

Keep it simple and easy to remember. When doing so, consider that you will also need a website, so you will want to pick a business name that you can get the domain name for, if at all possible. Domain names, like business names, should be easy to spell and not confusing to the customer. So, try to avoid weird spellings and dashes.

BestOutdoorLighting.com is already taken but try something like (your city) LEDLighting.com or (Your Name, if it's easy to spell) outdoorlighting.com. No matter what you choose, make sure it's simple and says what you do.

Next you will need to incorporate. You can be a sole proprietor, LLC or S Corp.

Here are some advantages/disadvantages of each:

Sole Proprietor:

Advantages:

The main advantage of a sole proprietorship is that the owner makes all the decisions without having to ask anyone what to do and therefore keeps all the profits from his or her business.

It's the easiest form of business to set up and can respond quickly to changes in the market for its products, goods, services, and information.

The profits are taxed once, as income to the owner.

Disadvantages:

If you're a solo flyer, you need to do all the work and handle an array of managerial skills. It's hard to do business while running a business. More businesses go out of business because of poor management than for any other reason.

Financing depends on the owner's credit rating and may be difficult to get.

It's hard to keep employees. They often leave once trained because they perceive that they have few opportunities for advancement, particularly in a family-run business and they may go out on their own after learning what you've got to teach them.

Limited Liability Corporation (LLC)

Advantages:

There's much less administrative paperwork and record keeping.

Limited liability means that the owners of the LLC, called "members," are protected from some liability for acts and debts of the LLC, but are still responsible for any debts beyond the fiscal capacity of the entity.

An LLC can elect to be taxed as a sole proprietor, partnership, S corporation or C corporation, providing much flexibility.

LLCs in some states can be set up with just one natural person involved.

LLCs in most states are treated as entities separate from their members, whereas in other jurisdictions case law has developed deciding LLCs are not considered to have separate juridical standing from their members. In other words, you're not usually personally liable for the debt of the business so your personal property may be safeguarded.

Disadvantages

Many states levy a franchise tax or capital values tax on LLCs. In essence, this franchise or business privilege tax is the "fee" the LLC pays the state for the benefit of limited liability. The franchise tax can be an amount based on revenue, an amount based on profits, an amount based on the number of owners or the amount of capital employed in the state, or some combination of those factors or simply a flat fee. In most states, however, the fee is nominal and only a handful charge a tax comparable to the tax imposed on corporations.

It may be more difficult to raise financial capital for an LLC as investors may be more comfortable investing funds in the better-understood corporate form with a view toward an eventual IPO.

LLC's are not required to have a board of directors or officers therefore the principals of LLCs can use many different titles — e.g., member, manager, managing member, managing director, chief executive officer, president, and partner. As such, it can be difficult to determine who actually has the authority to enter into a contract on the LLC's behalf.

Some creditors will require owners of up-and-starting LLCs to cosign for the LLC's loans, thus making the owners equally liable for the debt as the LLC is, and effectively removing the very purpose of forming an LLC: Limited Liability.

S Corp:

When forming an S-Corporation, there are rules that must be satisfied:

- The company must be a domestic corporation that elects to be treated as one.
- It cannot have more than 100 shareholders.
- The shareholders must be either individuals, estates, exempt organizations (such as a 501c3) or certain types of trusts.
- None of the shareholders may be nonresident aliens.
- It must have only one class of share. While there can be different voting rights for shares, they must all possess the same rights for distribution and events of liquidation.

Advantages:

As an owner, you can avoid having your business taxed twice. With a C-Corp, the profits are taxed first as the corporation and then all distributions are taxed. S-Corps avoid this.

The other advantage is that there are no self-employment taxes on distributions, which allow the shareholders to minimize their tax hit significantly.

Transfer of ownership is another advantage. If more than 50% of an LLC is transferred, the entire entity can be terminated, but shareholders of an S-Corp can sell their portion of the business without it resulting in any termination.

Disadvantages:

There can only be 100 shareholders. This isn't a big problem when you're first starting out, but if your idea is to eventually go public, there are likely to be many more than 100 shareholders. This can, therefore, interfere with your ability to raise money from a venture capitalist.

Another disadvantage is the "reasonable salary" requirement. The IRS gives little guidance on what constitutes reasonable salary, which can create a lot of ambiguity. However, the IRS has provided some factors that can be used to determine whether salary is reasonable. These include:

- Training and experience
- Duties and responsibilities
- Time and effort devoted to the business
- Dividend history
- Payments to non-shareholder employees
- Timing and manner of paying bonuses to key people
- What comparable businesses pay for similar services
- Compensation agreements
- The use of a formula to determine compensation

You can look at what similarly-situated employees are making. While it might be appealing to minimize salary in favor of more favorable distribution taxes, it's not worth dealing with the IRS.

Next you will need to be licensed and insured.

Licensing will vary from state to state. You will want to get a business license and be in compliance with state and local laws regarding selling your services. Remember, you are selling low voltage lighting and don't need to be an electrician.

Be sure to carry good insurance. We recommend at least one million dollars-worth of coverage. Most of the houses and businesses you will be lighting will be worth in excess of that figure. Don't be penny-wise and pound foolish when it comes to insurance. Shop around, ask questions, and get good liability coverage for you and your staff. People who own high dollar, luxury homes will want to see you're covered before letting you so much as set up a demo.

Align with industry groups & associations

Learn from others. Success leaves clues. Learn from people that have accomplished what you want to accomplish. You cannot expect to own a successful business without associating with the community of people that have been at this for many years. Build friendships with these people and they will be long lasting ones; they will be allies when you need them.

This is the secret sauce for success, building and connecting with the lighting design community. The foundation of Garden Light's philosophy is making these connections. We make those personal connections with and for our installers. Regardless of whether or not you work with us, adopt this philosophy and create bonds with this community.

One group you must join is The Association of Outdoor Lighting Professionals (AOLP)

The Association of Outdoor Lighting Professionals' mission is to promote and advance the landscape and architectural lighting industry for lighting designers and installers, distributors and business-to-business manufacturers.

AOLP was originally established in 2001 and is a trade association whose membership consists of contractors, manufacturers, lighting designers, landscape architects and distributors from all over the U.S. and Canada.

Getting Certified Through AOLP

What clearly identifies a professional from others in his or her industry? First and foremost are education and certification. AOLP has two excellent certification programs - Certified Low Voltage Lighting technician (CLVLT) and Certified Outdoor Lighting Designer Course (COLD).

Conference & Expo

AOLP's Annual Conference & Expo is known throughout the industry for its excellent educational sessions and speakers, as well as great opportunities for networking with vendors and members.

The AOLP offers its membership an advanced level of specialized training in landscape lighting design. This opportunity is the only one of its kind currently being offered. The goal is to develop this discipline by engaging lighting designers to analyze their work in peer group studies and through in-depth subject matter.

Design, or to be specific, landscape lighting design, is very subjective and cannot be tested upon. There are no set of rules to memorize, but there are a series of fundamental principles that are universally acknowledged to form the basis of "good and responsible" lighting design. Therefore, this program will insist on each participant contributing their photo work, thoughts, and questions to the entire group for everyone's learning benefit.

The AOLP believes in being proactive in their efforts by training its members in the practice of "good and responsible" landscape lighting design.

This sums up the programs purpose:

- To incorporate and ensure "good and responsible" lighting design practices
- To offer advanced levels of landscape lighting design training and instill professionalism to our designers
- To gain industry recognition and market exposure for our members and AOLP
- To understand and communicate the "emotional" impact of a landscape lighting design
- To address growing regulatory concerns and trade related issues

Low-Voltage CLVLT

Throughout the United States, there are no clearly-defined national standards for low voltage outdoor lighting. In most states, the test given to license low voltage contractors has little or nothing to do with the actual work that they perform. AOLP feels this lack of standards has a profound impact on the safety and quality of services that we provide.

AOLP has created a standardized certification test to address the lack of standards that presently exist. The Certified Low Voltage Lighting Technician (CLVLT) exam is administered by AOLP. The CLVLT exam measures the knowledge and capabilities of the applicants and is specifically for 12-volt systems.

The test consists of a written exam and seven half-hour labs. Upon receiving a passing grade, applicants are listed as Certified Low Voltage Lighting Technicians (CLVLT).

Set yourself apart from the competition, gain respect, acquire knowledge and invest in your future.

IES - Illuminating engineering society.

Who they are and what they do:

The IES offers multiple opportunities for the exchange of ideas and information and serves as a vehicle for its member's professional development and recognition. The IES is comprised of over 8,000 individual members all across the globe. Member of the IES are consultants, researchers, designers, educators, manufacturers and consumers who are involved in lighting by profession.

IES is the authoritative source of lighting standards. They offer opportunities to lighting professionals that are unlike anything in the industry. They create events and offer education and set lighting standards for the whole community. They keep a membership directory that helps lighting professionals connect with one another and the IES Career Center is the industry's best resource for top talent and job opportunities. IES keeps it members one step ahead with exclusive industry information. They create award-winning magazines and publications that all members have access to and most importantly, the EIS Lighting Handbook.

Once you become a member, you can achieve recognition from the IES whether you are an experienced professional in the industry or a novice. If you're going to be a lighting professional, joining is a must.

Successful lighting professionals must be able to incorporate into their work many new technological and scientific developments. Examples: solid state lighting sources, humans' perception of light as they age, sustainability and the integration of daylighting with electric lighting, the effects of light on human health, just to name a few. Clients rely on and expect lighting practitioners to know their specialties and to make well-informed decisions and recommendations. That's why the 10th edition of the new IES Lighting Handbook is an essential knowledge reference for anyone in lighting. The 10th edition brings together some of the best minds in the lighting community to present the current state of knowledge as it relates to lighting and lighting design. With reliable and comprehensive information in a single source, practitioners can approach projects with confidence.

Some other associations to look at and explore include:

US Department of Energy Program
Lighting Facts LED product Partner
DLC-Design Lights Consortium
IDA-Dark Skies Initiative
NGL-Award Next Generation Luminaires
ARRA
HG-No Mercury
ROHS Compliant-Reduction of Hazardous
Substances
GSA-Government Controls
IES
Florida Game and Wildlife

*Advance your knowledge of lighting -
Attend industry specific events like
our Garden Light LED Dealer Congress*

Here is some information about our 2018 Dealer Congress:

"You do not have to buy a franchise to build a great business." Building American Entrepreneurs.

Master turnkey, scalable business solutions with American-made products that will exceed your customers' expectations of quality and value.

Learning Objectives:

- Work with American Entrepreneur Mogul KEVIN HARRINGTON, original Shark from "Shark Tank"

- Become one of the most highly-valued and highly-paid LED lighting professionals in your local market
- Reach your business' peak performance with a roadmap that has been paved for over twenty-one years
- Breakaway strategy sessions with the most successful entrepreneurs in the LED lighting industry
- Gain insight on effective leadership, grow with other impactful industry persons of influence & adapt business success through education
- How to own your client, build referrals and attract the right customers that are profitable and fun to work with
- Perfect Your Pitch, convey Clarity, Credibility, the Problems you Solve, your Company's essence, and "The Why"
- Become the educator– Master LED Lighting technologies and how they relate to the products you sell
- Real-time tactical design to deliver installations that outshine your competitors

Create a strategic plan

A strategic plan is the foundation, pillar and compass that provides a company a roadmap. No company can begin its journey without that roadmap. It would be like saying you're going on a trip without the slightest idea where you're headed. A strategic plan is data driven and it is the cornerstone of the business. It provides a company empirical evidence to determine their position in the marketplace. The examples and references will be real time and time-tested strategies used by fortune 500 companies worldwide. For Garden Light, it was the Blue Ocean Strategy that changed the direction of a twenty-one-year mom and pop business like ours.

Expect making your strategic plan to require a minimum of 250-300 hours to complete before you will even begin profiting on the solutions you will uncover. Plan on three to four months of discovering, documentation, planning and execution before you even make a dollar.

Your plan should revolve around who you are, what benefits you plan to offer, what tools you plan to use. You need to know how you're going to kick ass and make people happy, what you want out of life, and what you plan to do for others.

Do you want to grow, expand, recruit, do all the things you have to do to scale up into a well-respected business? When the phone rings, and it will start ringing if you have a plan and execute it, will you be happy to answer it?

Building the kind of businesses that we work with, ones like our own, takes a tremendous amount of commitment. It starts with the strategic plan which is a living breathing document. You are going to change it over time, but without a plan your business will perish long before it can grow.

Before you decide to take this or any business on, be sure you have the backbone, fortitude and willingness to make a plan.

The chart below lays out all the things you need to consider when setting up a business.

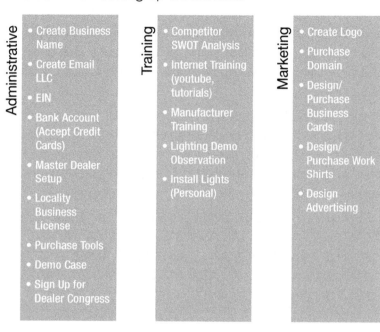

Administrative	Training	Marketing
• Create Business Name	• Competitor SWOT Analysis	• Create Logo
• Create Email LLC	• Internet Training (youtube, tutorials)	• Purchase Domain
• EIN	• Manufacturer Training	• Design/Purchase Business Cards
• Bank Account (Accept Credit Cards)	• Lighting Demo Observation	• Design/Purchase Work Shirts
• Master Dealer Setup	• Install Lights (Personal)	• Design Advertising
• Locality Business License		
• Purchase Tools		
• Demo Case		
• Sign Up for Dealer Congress		

Once you've established your name, gotten your business license and insurance and set up your corporation, you will get an Employer Identification Number (EIN). With that in place, you can open your business account and set up merchant services so you can accept payments. You may want to set up a Pay Pal account and you should get an online accounting software set up such as Quick books. Once you start to get really busy, you'll want to engage the services of a reputable accountant who will make sure your taxes are paid on time.

You're going to need to purchase tools. The most important tool in your arsenal will be your demo kit. You'll get that when you attend our Dealer Congress. With your demo kit, you'll be armed and ready to show potential clients what lighting their home really means. It's the most impressive way to show your stuff. Once they see what their home or business looks like lit up in the dark, they nearly always buy the product.

You will also be connected to the best American-made lighting fixture company available, Garden Light LED, and be able to offer our fixtures to your clients. You'll want to sell reliable products, ones that won't fail on your clients and have them calling you to complain. Garden Light LED products come with an unparalleled 20-year warranty. They're products you can sell with pride; American-made pride at that. You'll begin associating with other lighting professionals who have built multi-million-dollar companies. Surround yourself with people you want to be like. That's how you become the best you can be.

But you're also going to need marketing materials to be able to sell your services and reach the audience that wants and can afford you.

That's where we come in. Once you attend our Dealers Congress, you're eligible to become a Master Dealer and reap the benefits of our marketing team.

If you have a logo and are working on your branding, we will co-market your website and set your digital marketing in motion. If you don't have a website yet, we will build you one and help you become number one in your market area. Our team will handle your blogs, social media posting, search engine optimization, search engine listings, client reviews and much more.

In today's world, you need more than a business card and a few local ads to rise to the top. You need to reach people where they live. Yelp and Google reviews, social media presence, press releases, blog articles that show you to be the expert in the field and anything that will engage people quickly are all key marketing components. Clients must be able to find you from their phone and reach you with a touch of a finger.

Once your strategic plan is in motion, continuing education and certifications are a must. It's our mission in life to help educate, inspire and motivate our dealer partners. We're going to be there for you for the long haul, making sure that you succeed because your success is ours as well.

There are many steps to becoming a highly successful American entrepreneur. If you're willing to put in the time and effort up front by getting all your ducks in a row, you can own a company that brings in millions. We know. We've done it and helped lots of others to do it too.

Chapter 6

Creating and Establishing a Legacy Brand

Establishing your Company Brand

When we talk about "Brand" most people think in terms of logo, colors, slogans and marketing materials. That's all part of branding for sure and has to be considered. But the why behind all those choices is what branding is really about.

What does your logo say about the company you want to build? Why those colors? Your slogan should be more than just some clever phrase. People are smarter than that. Tell them what kind of business you represent. Show them your heart and your pride in what you do and they will flock to you. A slogan is something catchy people will remember, but your mission statement is the real meat of your branding.

Everything in the world is fueled by something. Cars run on gas; people need food, air and water to fuel the body.

Companies are living, breathing things. You need to know what fuels your company. That's the real essence of brand and, to truly succeed, that brand needs to carry through in everything you do.

It's important that you permanently establish your brand's attributes; what you stand for.

At GLLED we started by defining the words that said who we are.

Lifetime, Forever, Endlessly, Permanently, Perpetually, Enduringly, For Keeps were all words that resonated with us. "A Fixture for Life," became our brand slogan and we NEVER waver from our brand attributes in all aspects of our business. For Reto and I the What was easy. Make great fixtures. The Why evolved.

A fixture for life. Yes, it means the obvious. Lighting that won't quit on you, but it also means a fixture for "Life;" a fixture that will make life better for people. Not just the clients whose houses are safer, prettier, and more appealing to the eye. Lighting makes their lives brighter, if you'll pardon the pun, and that's a great thing, but we realized our Why was to light up the lives of our installer partners as well. Making the American dream come true means a better life for a lot of people; a fixture for life.

That's how we started to build our legacy brand and we want you to establish your own legacy.

What do I mean by Legacy Brand?

In my opinion, a legacy brand has four pillars.

1. It's generational, meaning it's a business that can be inherited by another through their discipline and hard work;

something that can be passed along to future generations, a business that is thinking of your children's children. This is becoming less and less the norm. Wouldn't it be great to have a business you can build and grow that your kids and grandkids could enjoy and reap great benefits from? That's what we want to build with you.

> Your brand should reflect your soul, core and essence - build a brand that resonates.

2. A legacy brand has Character. Legacy brands are cultural, lasting, and timeless, desirable, memorable, important and inspiring. A company that possesses character is attractive, appealing, and influences others to do the right thing or possibly to be more like them. It's is respected, carries merit, is trusted and associated with quality. Character gives people purpose.

3. It's a brand that represents quality. Doing what is right every time. It's fair. A legacy business has a good reputation and is known for quality. It has systems in place to ensure experience and service is consistent. We also believe that in today's technological world, a legacy brand is one that uses software to create and support these systems. It offers exceptional and memorable service that people talk about and refer to friends and family.

4. It's an organization that is humble and always learning, reading, educating and growing. It's a company that associates with other lighting professionals and shares experiences and best practices. When we help build a legacy brand for a business, they attend our Dealer

Congress because the owners of that business care about being the best and about taking time for training and communing with others in the industry.

Brand personality

What is it about your brand that conveys trust, competency and quality? When a person chooses your company to light their home or business, they are trusting you. They are saying, "come onto my property and make it beautiful, make it safe for my family, make it appealing to my customers, make it shine and reflect who I am or what my business does." It's not just a bunch of lights, it's "for life."

Product attributes

Think about the words that say what you want to convey to clients about your business and what you bring to the table. Here are some ideas.

What you will give them:
- Trustworthy, Reliable, Safe, High-quality,
  Simply the Best!

Why they will enjoy it:
- Safety, Elegance, Beauty, Notoriety.

You have to find your own words; your own what and why.

Visual brand language is the unique «alphabet» of design elements, such as shape, color, materials, finish, typography and composition – which directly and subliminally communicate a company's values and personality through compelling imagery and design style.

Design principles

Let's talk about color first.

Our minds are conditioned to respond to color. Red means stop, and green means go, right?

Color is the visual component people remember most about a brand. Defining shapes and symbols are the next thing we factor in followed by numbers and finally words. Yup, words are the last thing our brains take in.

Many of the most recognizable brands in the world rely on color as a key factor in the way they are perceived and recognized.

You may have noticed that FedEx has two different color schemes for their logo. Green represents their ground services; orange for their high speed, air transportation. Here are some ways colors are perceived:

Red – power, excitement, love

Orange – confidence, success, enthusiasm

Purple – creativity and playfulness

Green – Eco-friendly – growth - money

Blue – Honest, strong, trustworthy

Yellow – happy, cheerful, childlike

When you're choosing your colors consider how you want your company to be perceived?

Do you want to come off as powerful, down to earth, ecology-minded, honest, and dependable? Certain colors work well together. Hiring a graphic artist can sometimes be costly, but they can help with this.

Our Master Dealers get the advantage of working with the experts on our graphics team; another perk of the program.

Signature elements

Going back to FedEx, regardless of the color, the nearly subliminal use of the arrow elicits the feeling of forward motion. It's brilliant in its simplicity. McDonalds has the golden arches. Even if you don't read the words you see the red color and the arches, and you know what you're looking at.

If you're going to use a graphic element, it needs to reflect the message of your company. You don't have to have use a signature element but choose wisely if you want to do so. These are the things professionals can help with.

Font choice is part of your signature. Think about the coca cola logo. Simple right? Just the words in script font white and red.

But it's that font, that color of red; it's the most highly recognized logo in the world. No matter what elements they add behind it, bubbles, splashes, the bottle itself, you are not going to mistake that font for something other than Coke. It's not easy coming up with the right font. There are thousands and thousands of choices, some free, some you have to purchase to use.

Your brand should reflect your soul, core and essence - build a brand that resonates.

Let's look at a few very successful logos:

Target uses a red close to the red of Coke but it's a little brighter. Coke's red evokes a feeling of love. The target icon represents the bulls eye and the red is powerful.

Home Depot chose orange because it's one of the most recognizable colors. Orange says confidence and success. My favorite campaign of theirs was, "You can do it, we can help." It said we believe in you. You can complete that home project and we're right behind you.

Starbucks' constant main design ingredient is the black and white icon of the female. You don't need the green circle with the words Starbucks Coffee to know what company it represents. It's become part of the American fabric.

UPS' brown says you can depend on us. The shield is almost a badge of honor. It's meant to have you feel like they are taking care of your stuff when you ship it off someplace. They are grounded and reliable.

So, creating your brand is important. It's the essence of who you are, what your business represents and how you want the world to see you. We've built an entire team of marketing experts that are not only at our disposal but at the disposal of our partners; our installers who are part of our Master Dealer program.

Having a legacy brand and a plan allows you to recruit the right people in the future. Even if you're a one-person show or a little mom and pop operation, with the right legacy brand, you can grow and scale. You have a future that people will be attracted to.

Most business owners have no idea where to start when it comes to branding, color choices, design elements and fonts. No worries, we will be there with you step by step.

Chapter 7

The 4 Pillars of Digital Marketing

Some of you may watch the very popular TV show *Shark Tank* and you may have seen one of my mentors on that show, Kevin Harrington. Kevin believes you go digital or die. Kevin is the man behind the «As Seen On TV" campaign that launched major brands like OxiClean using infomercials, which is now worth around $200 billion. He's also one of the cofounders of the Entrepreneurs' Organization and has worked with founders to launch over 500 products that have brought in more than four billion dollars worldwide. He built all of these businesses and wealth through his use of digital marketing strategies. Not too shabby and luckily, he has become a friend and mentor to me. Like I said, I didn't go to college, but I have the smarts to surround myself with the right people. I make a point to learn from everyone I meet.

I met with Kevin at his home and explained in detail what I was doing for our Master Dealers and got his considered opinion. He explained that one of the big problems entrepreneurs run into is they get too comfortable. Kevin believes that small business owners need to aggressively use social media to continue reaching new customers and build relationships with existing ones. Otherwise, the business plateaus. That may be fine for some business owners, but we're here to grow the businesses we work with, not let them stagnate. The best way to do that in today's world is through aggressive use of social media and digital marketing.

Once your company is established, your branding is in place and you're ready to tackle business head on, you have the most daunting task of all.

Marketing!

We talked about the differences between traditional marketing and digital marketing. Now I want to go into detail about what digital marketing entails and the Why behind it.

I didn't understand the incredible power of digital marketing the first time it was presented to me. But that was a few years ago and I've since learned it was a mistake to not see the big picture it represents the first time someone tried to get me on board. I hope I can save you some steps and open your mind up to the possibilities. Change is hard to accept for many people and I get it, but if you embrace all that digital marketing can do for you, you will find yourself way ahead of the pack in the lighting industry. Many people in our industry want to do things the way they always have and that's fine, but it's not going to make you the dominant force in your area market. Digital marketing is what cuts the wheat from the chaff when it comes to becoming a top-seller and owning a million-dollar business.

The 4 Pillars of Digital Marketing

Let's look at the 4 pillars that make up the digital marketing strategy.

1. "Online Reputation"

How you are perceived as a business is super important in today's world. Reviews are everything. In order to get reviews and new customers, you need to be found. Then you need to manage your reputation.

A great digital marketing plan allows you to:

a. **Monitor, manage and market your online reputation** – Asking for reviews is the first step. Happy clients are happy to give reviews, but not nearly as often as unhappy clients are. Bad reviews aren't the end of the world, especially if you respond to them and offer to correct any issues that can be corrected.

b. **Get more sales by increasing trust** – The more business you do, the more business you should get. Do a great job for someone and they trust you. Once they trust you, they will recommend you. They will tell anyone that asks them about their wonderful new outdoor lighting, who did the great job, and how to reach out to that person; you!

c. **Get full control over your listing, content and brand online** – You need to be listed with Google and all search engines. Yelp is a huge factor too. Reputation sites like Angie's list are big factors as well. If you take charge of those listings, you can rest assured that your logo, colors, tagline, and all contact info are consistent and correct. Your website and social media links, address, operating hours, directions and phone numbers must be easily found in your listings. This is your digital real estate. Everything must be exactly the same and super concise. One little difference from listing to listing can throw things off. Expose your business and brand across Google, Yahoo and Bing. It's time consuming, but well worth the work.

With our reputation system, managing your reputation is easy. Why? Because we do nearly all of the work. We have a team for that and they know how to get you listed accurately EVERYWHERE.

2. "Social Media"

"Oh no! Don't tell me about social media."

I know, I know, you hear it all the time, but do you know why? Because it's true. It's the most powerful tool in your toolbox and often the least expensive.

What will using social media do for you and your business?

a. **Grow your local fan base.** People are spoiled by the ease in which they can get answers to questions now. You want a reliable plumber? Just shout out on Facebook and twenty friends will respond with their personal experiences. Even though the internet connects the world, people want to know what's going on in their own backyard. There are groups and pages you can "advertise" on in every corner of the world that are geographically specific. Join and like them all and interact with the folks who check in daily.

b. **It's a source for real-time leads.** People ask, "Who does great outdoor lighting?" And everyone responds. People like to show that they're in the know. Most people like being helpful. Be the company they recommend every time someone asks.

c. **Share relevant content across Facebook and Twitter with the push of a button.** Share your knowledge and you become the "expert." You can write posts and articles and you can send those to all your social media platforms at once if you learn how. With the available software you can schedule a post; then set-it-and-forget-it. You can even set all your posts for the whole week in one place and the software will do the job of doling them out as you request.

d. **Monitor changes in Facebook and Twitter.** Social media is an ever-changing world, especially Facebook. The rules change but if you know how to navigate the changes, you'll just keep getting attention. Post to multiple social channels too, not just Facebook. Pinterest and Instagram are all about the visuals. We sell lighting so… DUH! These platforms can be big winners for your company and get some real engagement going.

e. **Track growth across channels from a single dashboard.** Analytics is the name of the game. Once things are set up in the appropriate software, you can see what people are paying attention to, how many new people are liking your page or following your blog posts. Once you start to form a picture of the kind of people that are watching you, you can start to reach out to them and glean business from the connections you make.

f. **Start conversations with customers and offer incentives to buy.** Interact with them. Ask questions, run contests, offer value and reasons why they should choose you.

3. "Search Engine Optimization" (SEO)

I know you hear the term all the time but here is what it really means.

Search engine optimization is the process of improving the ranking of your web pages on search engines such as Google, Yahoo and Bing versus your competition. It's a science and not an easy one. It requires knowledge of best keywords and phrases that a potential client will be "searching" for.

The actual code of a website is a factor. Google knows if the code is what developers refer to as "clean code." So, having a well-constructed website is essential. Today Google will not allow you to rank high in searches if your website is not built in "responsive design." Simply put, that means that your site needs to size up and down to fit properly on something as small as your phone and as big as the largest desktop monitor and all sizes in between. The site needs to "respond" to those different sizes. Your potential client is looking for you on his or her phone, more than likely. Your site needs to be very accessible on that phone.

Oh no! Don't tell me about social media.

Constant movement and updating of a site shows the search engines that the site is alive and active. That's a big reason why some websites come up near or at the top of the page in their search category. This is why blogging is so important. Fresh content every week means higher ranking, not to mention positioning you as an expert. SEO will give you high visibility and ranking, more traffic to your website and a higher probability of receiving new leads and booking appointments for demonstrations.

When you work with Garden Light LED and become one of our Master Dealers, we optimize your website for specific keywords along with location information (keyword examples are LED lighting, outdoor LED lighting and landscape lighting). Location words are names of the towns, cities and areas in which you work and are seeking work.

If you already have a website, we will co-market your website with ours. If you don't have one, we will build you a co-branded website and create a SEO strategy for the site and your target market. All of our Master Dealers websites carry the Master Dealer Designation for your market area. It's synonymous with quality and attaches you to our well-known and respected legacy brand.

Here are some examples of co-marketed sites we've created and maintain for our partners:

Parkhurstoutdoorlighting.com
Apollooutdoorlighting.com
DanAllenlandscapelighting.com

This is all part of the deal when you work with us. We don't just want you to succeed, we want you to dominate the market in your area and we know how to make that happen.

4. "Customer Relationship Management (CRM)"

Ifyouwanttogrowamulti-million-dollarbusiness,youneed to get leads and then turn those leads into sales. All the tools we talked about above should bring in leads. But now what? You have to manage those leads, set appointments, talk to the client, set up the lighting demo and then… follow up. The real money is in the follow up.

Here are the steps involved with our CRM.

a. Manages the leads and prospects that the marketing platform generates

b. Those Leads will filter directly into the CRM tool

c. Turns more of them into long-term customers

d. Guides your interactions with new prospects and leads

e. Stores the important data about customers' history with the dealer

f. Helps to establish, maintain and improve business relationships with customers

How many times have you lost a lead because you didn't remember to follow up with the person or lost the job because you waited too long to get back to them? It's hard to keep track of leads, harder to set appointments, follow-up, and remember to keep in touch with them. Any customer can be a repeat customer. People move, their friends need lighting, they buy a second home that needs lighting or a new business. There are dozens of reasons why they may come back to you, but only if you do a great job from the get go. That means being easily found and reached, getting back to them promptly, setting up and making it to appointments, doing a great demo for them and then a great install. If you're a one-person business, that's hard to keep track of alone. As you grow and have employees, you get even busier, so you then need someone to keep track of all this. We have a system for that. We take that burden off your shoulders, so you can do what you do best; install great outdoor LED lighting.

All this takes persistence and patience. I have thought long and hard about all of this, knowing quitting is not an option. What I've learned is that even though all of this sounds daunting, maybe even impossible, it's not. Not if you automate your operations and streamline your systems. People get frustrated and quit when they realize the amount of work that goes into all that is digital marketing. We know that, which brings us back to our What and Why.

Our What is growing American businesses and American entrepreneurs. Our Why is the knowledge that we can improve the lives of our installers and help them improve the lives of other people; their families, their employees and their families, and the clients' lives, homes and families. It's a chain reaction.

No one wakes up in the morning and says I'd rather be posting on Facebook or writing blog articles and press releases rather than do the work I'm passionate about, unless you're Donald Trump who seems to enjoy tweeting more than being President. However, digital marketing folks are passionate about digital marketing. Our team of digital marketing experts are passionate about it. This allows you to wake up and do your job; lighting designing and installing.

Our marketing team is constantly creating relevant content for our businesses. We take that content and repurpose it for our dealer's local markets. We create high-quality corporate videos on specific topics that are tied to the Garden Light LED corporate brand. Those can be used on all of our Master Dealer's co-marketed websites because they are using the GLLED products and carry the legacy brand and the Master Dealer Designation.

This kind of content is invaluable. Professionally produced videos, blogs, and web content bring attention to the website and therefore the company. We create blogs and videos that solve problems, incorporate innovative ideas, show expertise and give value so they get read and watched. All the content can be related to our dealer's local market. We add the logo, company name and appropriate links to the blogs that are placed on the co-marketed websites and pushed out to social media. We attach you to shoulder industries, thus getting the attention of their customers. Writing articles about how lighting works with landscaping, pools and bridges attaches you to those businesses and anyone that's interested in those subjects. Lighting for weddings and events grabs that rather large audience and shows you to be an expert on lighting for those industries. Anywhere lighting can be used, we can blog about it and get traction. This is how you build SEO value and we do all of that for our installer partners.

Your head is probably swimming from all the information on Digital Marketing. Yes, it's daunting, but we've got this. All you have to do is believe in yourself, your American dream, and let go of any resistance you might be feeling. We're here with you every step of the way.

Congratulations, you made it through the most difficult part of the book – take a selfie and send it to me in an email.

Chapter 8

Positioning Yourself as a Lighting Designer

Most people don't wake up one morning and think, "I should be a lighting designer." It isn't a common career choice for young people like doctor, lawyer or engineer. It isn't a career that one thinks of in terms of a franchise, like buying a cleaning or pest control business. But it's a great career and when you work with Garden Light LED you don't need to buy a franchise to own a lighting design business. We know what it takes to position yourself as an expert in lighting design and we can help you get there.

Positioning yourself as a lighting designer rather than a lighting installation company is the most critical and lucrative differentiator your company can make. You have to consider everything from the quality of the lighting fixtures to the colors you choose. It's thinking about the whole picture; what elements on a property to light and how to light them. This knowledge comes with education, training, and time in the field. You must always be learning and growing.

Architectural Lighting Designer vs. Lighting Installation Company – a little story.

When reaching out to clients I often go on their websites and investigate their work. I'm always interested to learn how lighting professionals began and how they got into the lighting business in the first place. I met with the owner of a lighting company out of California and, as I often did, I took some time to discuss his site and the work that he was most proud of. In the majority of the photos in his portfolio, I noticed that the architecture was not lit. Image after image, I saw that, sadly, only the landscape and trees were lit. I asked the gentleman if there was a reason why none of the architecture was lit. He quickly replied, that's my style. I only light the landscape and the trees. After further inquiry on the lighting products and suppliers he chose, he informed me that he uses Kichler fixtures with LED bulb technology. Now I was completely confused. This company was based in California where integrated technologies and adoption led the way for the rest of the nation. He owns a lighting business in California, yet his lighting designs do not include lighting the architecture, which is the most important part of the project and he is using dated LED bulb technology. Kindly, I replied, "I am surprised you're still in business." Integrated LED technology cannot be beat in terms of efficiency, consistent light output and desirability and you're choosing not to light the most important element of the design, the architecture itself.

In my opinion, this is a case of someone that owns a lighting installation company, not someone that chooses to be a lighting designer.

Right from the get-go, you need to decide you're going to be an architectural lighting designer, not only someone that knows the ins and outs of setting up nice lighting, but someone that looks at a piece of property and sees what if could look like if properly lit. You have to be a bit of a dreamer, a visionary.

> Every space in the world is lit in some way, even if only by the moon and the stars.

We often hear statements like, "I've been in this business for years. I know what I'm doing. I don't need to learn anything new. Just give them lights and they're happy."

Nothing could be further from the truth. Lighting makes dark spaces safer. It creates moods; happy, joyful, quiet, contemplative, sexy, bold, brash, fun. Every space in the world is lit in some way, even if only by the moon and the stars.

Being a lighting designer means more than just plopping lights down around a property and connecting wires. Lighting is everything. It's an amazing thing to take a dark space and bring light to it; to make it feel safe, warm, exotic, cool, exciting. Most people don't think about light the way a lighting designer does. People have to see something go from dark to light to understand the full value of what we do; what we are capable of doing for them, their home, their business, their family.

Collaborative Design

One thing Reto and I believe in fully is the collaborative design process. Yes, you're the expert, and you want to guide the client, but to be the leader in your field you need to get the client involved in the process. Take time to get to know them. Ask questions.

Who lives in the house? Do they have kids, pets, elderly parents? Do they entertain a lot? Have a set of questions you routinely ask, a questionnaire of sorts, that will help you to know what kind of client you're dealing with.

A collaborative design includes all of the decision makers and is a wonderful tool to ensure the desired look and overall project turns out the way both you and the home or business owners envisioned. Remember, it is critical to offer your client a free, no obligation, lighting demo. This creates an experience this customer will not get from your competitors. Over the years, hundreds of lighting professionals have told me that they have been in business forever, they have a great reputation, and they do not do lighting demos. This is an enormous mistake and those companies are leaving a tremendous amount of money behind.

Flip the Switch - The Power of the Lighting Demo

Remember Clark Griswold of *National Lampoon's Christmas Vacation* and his Christmas lights? He couldn't get them to go on. The house was dark and disappointing, but when they flip the switch and lights do come on finally, they're amazing, although blinding.

You don't need or want to blind your prospective customers, but you want that same feeling of total awe and amazement when you flip the lights on and their house goes from total darkness to beautifully lit. Fortunately, you can't blind people with LED lights. But the more lights, the better.

If you Invest the time to show them what they've been missing, they simply can't say no to your proposal. When we do the demo onsite and show them what it can do to enhance their property, 99% of the time we leave with a signed contract. We leave with a check and an install date too.

Choose a small area, a segment of the house and blast it with lights. You have to be strategic and maximize the opportunity to sell more lights. Plan out and stage a section of the house to blow them away with lights and make them want the entire property lit that way.

The competition is fierce. Do something your competitors won't take the time or effort to do. Light the customers world. Show them what your expertise will bring to their lives.

You know that you need to study and learn. You need to know what fixtures are best in what application. Show them things like the difference between a 3 dimensional and a 4 dimensional effect and how more than one light on a tree makes a huge difference. We work with our Master Dealer installers to continually educate them and help them learn and grow. Lighting is always changing. New technologies happen, and you have to stay up with what's new, hot and cutting edge. We can help with that. The main thing is, grab a hold of your equipment and play with it. Okay, you know I mean the lights, right? The more you try out the lights, experiment with what they can do, the better you will get at this. Put them up against trees and architecture, add lights, and try out different fixtures, colors and textures. Light is so powerful and can create anything. The more you understand about it the better you will be at creating compelling experiences for customers and the more sales you will close with ease.

When you attend our Dealer Congress, you're going to learn a lot. You're going to hear talks and meet up with industry giants, people that know what's new and exciting in the lighting industry and you're going to leave with your very own Demo Case. Our Start Up Demo Case includes $2000 worth of a variety of fixture finishes, optics, different voltage output products, about 20 in all, a battery pack and everything you need to do a basic demo for a client. You can set up a lighting demo in minutes and give the potential client a taste of what they're in for. It's a great starting point for anyone who is beginning in this business.

When you realize how critical lighting demos are, and how much they drive sales and increase your bottom line, you're going to want our ShowTime Closer. It contains 100 lights and all the tools to show what a total lighting system will look like. And guess what? It will take around the same 15 minutes to set up. Reto created this kit to put this great tool in our installers' hands. No other manufacturer offers this. The system is completely plug and play and all you need to do is pop the appropriate fixture into place. The runs and the wire are created so there is no twisting or turning. It's a quick connect. It's all preset. Your job is to design the lights. The kit makes it easy to show off your design in minutes.

What you have to ask yourself is, "is that 15 minutes of my life worth spending to get higher paying contracts, close deals nearly 100 percent of the time, and make me the go to guy for lighting design in my neck of the woods?"

We know that it is, but you have to be willing to do the work. We know how lighting is sold. Reto has been doing it for 20 years.

Create a Lighting Experience for your Customers

Selling lighting is no big secret; it must be demonstrated and sold. When the lights go on, the client has an overwhelming experience; seeing what was once completely dark in a whole new light. Let's face it, the single largest investment most of us will make in a lifetime is our home, our sanctuary, the place we rest after a long day at work, where our children experience their childhood memories.

Over the past two decades, we have perfected and trained hundreds of entrepreneurs on how to successfully sell LED lighting and how to create an incomparable "WOW" experience for their customers each and every time. All of the LED lighting professionals that lead the industry in volume and service provide their customers what most competitors will not take the time to invest in, "A Nighttime Demo."

When you provide your customers a nighttime demo experience, it is all about the VALUE rather than the features and benefits. Features and benefits are felt first hand when they simply see the results.

If you get what we're talking about and will do the hard work, the money will come. Ask the right questions. Set up the appointment. Do the demo and make the quote.

Customer interface:

Be personable. Leave all your annoyances of the day in the truck and get out with a big smile on your face. Be polite and enthusiastic. If you're excited, they will be too. Don't let them think that your coming out to their home or business after the rest of the world is done for the day is a bother for you. They'll know. Think about realtors that work Sundays and holidays, showing houses, often for people that don't buy. That's part of that business. Would you rather be stuck behind a desk or at some job you hate because you get to watch TV after dinner instead of making some family or business owner freak out about how amazing their property looks with true lighting design? I didn't think so. The great thing about the lighting demo is that it does a lot of the work for you. You just have to show up, know your fixtures and have a plan. In 15 minutes or less, you will turn their black, blank canvas into a lighting work of art and they will be impressed and ready to buy. You have to see what lights can do for you to appreciate them. It's not something you can envision in your head. Once you have the property lit, let them take the time to walk around, ask questions and move lights around if they want to see something different. Give them your time and attention. This is one thing they can't order on Amazon and have dropped off on the doorstep the next day. This requires something really special… You!

Chapter 9

Making the Sale

First and foremost, always be selling.

There was a gentleman by the name of Paul who I met at a sandwich shop here in Tampa. We began talking and sharing what we both did for a living. I was excited when Paul told me that he and his partners were an unusual group of investors that are in the property management business and that they owned several office buildings and managed even more. This group of investors were involved in several new projects and were purchasing existing buildings throughout the Tampa Bay area with plans of rapid growth for the future. I told him we were a local manufacturer of outdoor LED lighting and invited him to tour the factory and see what we are all about. He accepted my invitation and came over to the office. We walked him through the facility and listened as he shared all the projects he was involved in and driving with his team. The opportunities were endless; this group of mavericks love lighting and wanted to light up each of the executive spaces with LED lighting for security, but they were also interested in color branding and creating a recognizable brand with distinctive lighting solutions. All of that because I love what we do so much that I tell everyone about it. Given the opportunity, I always mention my company and the great work we do. You never know who you might meet, even in the most unlikely places, like waiting for your turkey sub to be made. Shout out from the rooftops that you are a lighting design professional. Never hide your "light" under a bushel. Talk to everybody. Shyness gets you no business. Everybody needs lighting of some sort or they know someone who does.

There is definitely a science to quoting a lighting system and closing the sale. It's not just a matter of doing the demo and telling them the price.

Bidding and offering a lighting package is as much of an art form as the lighting design and demo experience. I have seen guys talk themselves right out of the sale or offer too many manufacturers and fixture options to the customer. This causes confusion and gives the client mixed signals and too many decisions to make. The process needs to be smooth and simple. You're the expert. This is where working with one LED lighting manufacturer you can trust comes in. You know your cost and margins upfront and this allows you to be a better entrepreneur. It will allow you to make quick decisions if you need to negotiate to ensure you get the sale. Our installers work on a 60% margin, meaning they generally see a profit of 60% when they use our products. This gives you some wiggle room. If you have a client that needs a little better price point, you can negotiate down to a 50% or even 40% margin and still be making a great profit. Sometimes price is the issue but not always.

Let's look at the overall process of making a sale.

Scheduling:

Once you get the lead for the client, you have to start with scheduling. Get them on the phone and ask all the things you need to know about them to start to work on a lighting plan in your mind. Thanks to Google Earth, you might even be able to see their home on your computer, maybe even while you're talking to them. If you can take a look at the home or business before you do the demo, more's the better, but if you get enough info from them you may not need to. The main thing in setting the schedule is that it needs to be at least an hour after sunset for maximum darkness. Arrive when it's still light enough for you to set up and then be prepared for the property owners to see the design after dark. You need to know that any and all decision makers will be home to see your handiwork. You don't want to interfere with dinner or be lighting the house like *Christmas Vacation* during bedtime for small children. Let's not be the Griswolds. Establish a time that's good for them and dark enough to blow their minds.

Consultative selling

Here is a list of great questions to ask before you meet with them for their awesome night demo.

1. Do you have prior experience with outdoor lighting?

2. If yes to #1, what did you like about it and were there any disappointments?

3. If yes to #1, what would have improved your experience with these lights?

4. If yes to #1, confirm likes and dislikes along with desired improvements.

5. What is your primary goal for this project?

6. Do you have any examples, photos, web pages, etc. that are good examples of what you are trying to accomplish?

7. What would a perfect lighting design look like to you?

8. What is your time frame for getting your project completed?

9. What is your expectation with regard to a budget and what do you hope that budget will cover?

10. Were you aware that the average outdoor lighting system fails after a year or two? That's where you explain to them that Garden Lights products have been designed and manufactured to last decades – 20-year guarantee baby!

We have perfected the customer qualifying, lighting demo and end-user experience for over twenty-one years. These strategies are time tested and proven to be successful if implemented and not deviated from.

Let's review the process:

a. Qualify. Qualify. Qualify. – Google the address and see if they have existing lighting, what they like and dislike about lighting, if they ever had a professional lighting system installed, what is their budget, make sure both decision makers are present.

b. What is their timeframe?

c. Once you get to the house, do an inventory – do they have nice cars, well-manicured property, cheap lighting fixtures?

d. Provide a lighting demo. A lighting demo is an experience that you excitedly create for each of your customers and almost guarantees the sale when conducted correctly.

Point of sale

The sale really begins when you pick up the phone, intently listening to your prospect, qualifying the customer, setting up a nighttime demo, verifying that all the decision makers will be present to see your demo, and preparing well for that demo. If you know what matters to them, you can plan to do a demo that will blow their minds.

Once you finish that demo, you have them right there in their home or at their business. Don't wait to close. ABC - Always Be Closing. That kick ass demo you gave them was part of closing. In fact, everything you've done to this point was part of closing the deal; the phone conversation where you asked them about their needs. Closing. The excited attitude you showed them when you arrived. Closing. Setting up the demo. Closing. Answering all their questions and making adjustments... Closing!

The lighting demo is an experience for the customer; they say a picture paints a thousand words. Imagine what an actual experience does for your customers.

Dynamic quoting:

Good, Better, Best.

Once all the questions have been answered, here comes the part lots of people dread. Pricing. If you're lighting their property with our ShowTime Closer, you've most likely shown them what 100 or so lights can do for their property. You've shown them Garden Light LED's fixtures, which are the best and will last 20 years or more. Start with the big price. The one with all the bells and whistles; solid brass. Don't assume they won't go for it. If you start with the lower priced options, they get that idea in their heads. It's harder to work up to the best if you start with the good.

You can tell them about the good and better options if they balk at or simply can't afford the best. Be ready to do that but be hopeful that you won't have to. If you need support, we will be there to help you, but ultimately you have to have the drive and spirit to carry this through; to make the sale, to become a true Lighting Designer, not just a person that installs lights.

We will explain good, better and best quality in a later chapter in detail.

Creating the proposal

Listening to the customer after you have provided the nighttime demo experience is the beginning of creating a light proposal for your customer.

When you sell our products, that 60% profit margin gives you plenty of room to play. Give them the top price and then shut up. Don't start offering them too many choices or start lowering your price because you assume their silence means they think it's too much to spend.

Once you present the cost - don't speak. He who speaks first, loses. Let the client digest exactly what you just told them, let it sink in before you begin back peddling. Once they are in the lit environment, processing what you have just delivered, they are contemplating the value and how they are going to pay for it or perhaps justify the cost or expense. Is it going to improve their life so much so that they can justify the cost, and most importantly, can they quantify the VALUE of the solution for years to come?

DOES LIGHTING SOLVE problems for people? YES! That is why your pitch is imperative, and you must have an awesome pitch. It's my belief that lighting can increase your lifespan. It brings peace and harmony to your life. Make bold statements. You want to live longer? Get landscape lighting. Happiness equals long life. Check out the stats on that one.

When I say, have a pitch, I mean a competitive advantage of some sort, or even just a specialty. In other words, be unique. That is why people will choose you over somebody else and you can avoid just offering another commodity service. Communicate with clarity what your business does, add credibility to why you do it better than your competitors, state the problems your company resolves, establish the essence of why you do what you do, and how that service translates to the customer.

It's very important to put the fixtures in the client's hand, let them feel the quality of the material and inform them of the manufacturing process. This allows them to decide for themselves and make a decision to make an investment in a lighting system and YOU. You've lit their house up and wowed them. Now you hand them a top-quality light and tell them that light comes with a 20-year guarantee and they can feel it because the fixture in their hand, the one made in America by Garden Light LED, FEELS like MONEY! They're excited now, and you should be too.

Don't take your foot off the pedal. Don't tell them you'll get back to them with a quote. Be prepared to give them one right then and there. Have all the paperwork ready for them. Make it easy for them to sign that contract, write that check, and have your calendar in your hand so you can arrange their install. Or, if you're part of the twenty-first century, have your operating and invoicing software in your hand. Make it easy for them to sign right up.

Shyness gets you no business.

You've got them ready to purchase. I promise you they will want you to leave the lights there that night. They want to see their house lit up that way every night. Don't allow time for buyer's remorse. Make the sale then and there.

Very few people are born salesmen. It's a learned skill and it takes a commitment to constant education on the subject. Read books, take seminars, go to workshops. Find a mentor that can help you grow in this effort. I highly recommend studying recognized and renowned sales trainers. My favorite is Jeffrey Gitomer. He is the author of 17 books on sales. You'll learn a ton by reading his books and watching his videos.

Check out his book, *How Not to Suck at Sales.* Trust me; this guy is the go-to guru on the subject of sales. He has taught me so much and if you take the time, he'll teach you as well.

Let's recap

Here is a step-by-step scenario of what a quality lighting design and quoting experience should look and feel like. It's something I learned when Kyle McKelvy spoke at our Dealer Congress in 2016. It stuck because it's good.

The Sales Process and Where the Demo Fits (12 Steps)

1. Attitude
2. Greeting
3. Fact Finding
4. Design & Proposal Write Up
5. Company Presentation
6. Fixture Presentation & Selection
7. Design and Proposal Presentation
8. Negotiation
9. OFFER A NIGHTTIME DEMONSTRATION
10. Ask for The Sale
11. Delivery/Installation
12. Follow-up, Follow-up, Follow-up

Once you get the sale, and you will if you do all the things we've discussed, there's one more thing you need to do.

Ask for referrals

My friend's parents ran a motel when I was young, and from them I learned a lot about customer relations. More than 65% of the reservations at the motel came from customers who came back year after year. And the number one source of new customers was through referrals. As they built a relationship with each guest, they got know their extended families and friends, and they were not shy about asking for a referral.

It's was as easy as saying, "Wouldn't it be nice if you all vacationed together next year?" Or, "Why doesn't your cousin Joe who is staying down the road, stay here? It would be much more convenient for you all, and it would be wonderful to have him."

It's nice when clients make referrals on their own, but as a rule you can't expect them to connect the dots between the people they know who might need your services and you. Ask questions and ask for referrals.

The Fortune is in the Follow-up.

It's also in the drive to sell, the willingness to do the demo, the courage to set the price and ask for the sale. We can help you with all of that and more, but it's up to you to put in the hard work.

Chapter 10

The Benefits of Outdoor Lighting

No matter what the goals are for an outdoor space, there are compelling reasons why your clients should invest in a quality outdoor LED lighting system. When speaking to clients, it's part of your job to not only explain how your lighting design will enhance the overall beauty and value of their home, but also to tell them of the many additional benefits outdoor lighting brings.

Let's look at the most important benefits of LED Lighting.

Beauty

Agreeably, first and foremost, is straight up beauty.

After dark, nothing transforms a home more than perfectly balanced lighting. I cannot stress enough how valuable the nighttime demo is when talking about pure esthetics. Show, don't tell. Yes, you can have a portfolio; in fact, that's a must. And having pictures and even video on your website is a great way to show off your work. But those homes are not their home. Show them how unbelievably beautiful their home is going to look with LED lighting design. Don't just light the trees and shrubbery. Light the architecture. Show them how stunning lighted walkways, decks, patios, and pool areas will look when properly and colorfully lit.

Security

Other than the sheer beauty LED lighting brings, the next and perhaps biggest benefit to remind them of is security. Intruders are far more likely to target dark, unlit homes. Plus, a well-lit exterior can help prevent falls or other injuries that result from low-lit environments. Ask them if they have elderly parents or loved ones that live with them or visit often. Do any of them come home late at night from work or activities? Outdoor lighting allows them to have that beautiful landscaping but lit well so that intruders won't be lurking behind a shrub, bush or clump of trees. There's no way to hide in that environment. Pool areas that are well lit mean a much safer way to enjoy night swims and parties.

Fully utilizing your space

When the sun goes down, that doesn't mean you have to go inside. A well-thought through outdoor LED lighting system can extend the hours your customer and his or her family can linger outside. Remind them that they can eat outdoors or just sit and enjoy the night and their beautiful lighting. Their home may look like a million dollars during the day but when lit, it will look like 2 million at night, when you're actually there to enjoy it.

Here are some types of lighting that you can offer clients that offer excellent benefits.

Moon lighting

This type of lighting gives the illusion of moonlight shining down through the trees. It is more of an atmospheric style of lighting, although it can also serve the practical purpose of bringing light to a dark area. If they have a large property, this means they can take a romantic stroll in their gardens or plan an intimate dinner for two in soft, charming lighting.

Security lighting

This is the strategic placement of no-glare fixtures specifically designed to illuminate dark or less-visible areas of a property. While it can also be beautiful, it has a more functional purpose.

Let the kids play in the yard or in the pool after dinner. Lighting means safety and more peace of mind.

Step lighting

This is a type of lighting used to illuminate a single step, or a group of steps, to improve the safety of those walkways. This is especially important as family members age. Remind them that if they plan to stay in their home long term, the older one gets, the more difficult it is to navigate steps. The lights you're giving them will last 20 years, so their steps are good for a couple of decades. Step lighting is also important for visitors. People coming to your home may not realize how to navigate your steps in the dark. That's the stuff of lawsuits. Properly placed step lighting can avert those issues.

Functional can also be beautiful

When thinking about outdoor space, there are a few things to keep in mind:

1. You will want to ensure you give the customers comprehensive coverage of the areas that are most important to them. This includes the outdoor spaces they will use on a regular basis, the unique features of their landscape you want to highlight for them and the areas they tell you they would like to enjoy more regularly.

2. Think in terms of effects, not fixtures. The purpose of outdoor lighting is to highlight the beauty of the home and landscape, not to look at the fixtures themselves. When possible, fixtures should be hidden, keeping the focus on the area being illuminated. When the fixtures can't be hidden, they should be an aesthetically pleasing design, shape and finish that compliments the overall look and feel of your design plan. Garden Light LED fixtures are the highest-quality LED lights on the market today and are aesthetically pleasing to the eye. In fact, we've been told that they are sleek and sexy.

3. Consistency. You will want the right equipment and placement to ensure that the brightness levels of your lighting remain consistent throughout the entire area. You don't want to have pockets of bright light and darkness. This is why they've chosen you, the expert lighting designer, to help them. It's your job to ensure that every light is placed to deliver the peak illumination. Low-quality or even average-quality LED lights are moderately to extremely inconsistent in the light levels and patterns and can even flicker. Lights in color, or even white, can have inconsistent color temperatures, light levels, patterns, hot spots and

hues and flickering issues. This is where a Garden Light LED light distinguishes itself from all others in quality and consistency.

Everyone's property is unique. Show them what you can do for them in the night demo and ask for their feedback. Once you get the job, you will want to be sure you're giving the client the most bang for their buck. If safety is their highest priority, make sure that every nook and cranny is lit, that the steps are easily navigated, and the pool is lit for safety and enjoyment. If

Show, don't tell

they are the romantic type, give them ambiance; moonlight effects, soft colors and warm glows.

If they have kids, make lighting that will allow them to have fun around the yard while also feeling safe and secure. Beauty first, but safety and functionality fall in right behind and perhaps even go hand in hand, depending on the job.

If you're tasked to light businesses, many of the benefits will be the same. In some cases, beauty might be traded for attention-grabbing. Lights will attract different customers for different reasons. For example, a nightclub will want a different style of lighting than say a real estate office.

Both businesses want to attract clients, and both will note safety as an issue, but for different purposes. A nightclub needs to be well lit for safety so that patrons don't trip (again lawsuits are no fun), so that there are no dark corners where someone could pull a patron into a bad situation and even so that law officials can identify the building quickly should they need to be called.

A real estate or other such office will want to have lighting that discourages would-be thieves or vagrants from breaking in or lurking about. Also, night lighting is helpful should the owner or agents need to return to the office after dark to work on something for or even with a client. More light, less risk.

All businesses, whether they're open after dark or not, have reasons to want to be seen. Most businesses want to have some illumination of the property, even if they're a 9 to 5 operation. People driving by in the evening after business hours will see their building and their signage and make note of that business for future reference. If the building sits in darkness half the time, they let money go out the window. Businesses need to be visible and, better still, attractive at all times.

Color is going to be a big issue with businesses. We will discuss color in another chapter more fully but know that color choice for a business is crucial as it can say so much about the culture of that business. Different colors will attract different clientele.

Lighting is a science. The more you study and learn, the more valuable you will be and the more lucrative your business will become.

Chapter 11

Types of Lighting

When you know how to light properties, you're simply going to make money. The name of the game is light everything and light it well. The more areas of a property there are to light, the bigger the opportunity for you to increase the scope of the project.

Don't just light the TREES! Light the house, the walkways, the fences, the driveway. Make sure when you quote a lighting design for a business that you add into that quote the entire parking lot, the fencing and shrubbery around it. There are all types of lights. Use them all. Fill in the spaces with light that is appropriate for those spaces.

There are lots of kinds of lighting but there are three main categories they can be lumped into: Architectural, Landscaping and Perimeter. Most of what I'm about to tell you is basic information but I want to be sure you're clear on what you can offer and how you can increase your bottom line on any contract by offering EVERYTHING!

Architectural

If architectural lighting is your business, you need to be savvy and smart in all aspects of your business. It's not just make a sale and place lights. You need to be an expert at installation, core drilling, concealing wire, matching finishes, placing lights and creating lighting effects no one else has ever dreamed of designing.

To create aesthetic appeal with the architecture you're lighting, your job, as a lighting designer, is to raise the level of attractiveness of the design. Should your lighting should be subtly blended into the background or stand out boldly? What kind of emotions should the lighting evoke? How can you elevate those emotions? If the structure you're lighting needs to feel majestic, create lighting that makes it feel big and powerful with dynamic lighting. If it needs to feel warm, make it glow with softness. Talk to the owners. They have a personality and so does the home they've chosen or the culture of the business they own. Reflect that personality and you have a customer for life and a referral partner who will sell you to everyone they know. Learn to play with colors, shadows and textures. As a lighting professional, this is your greatest opportunity on every project. It's where you will host the most lights. It's the property owners biggest point of pride. It's what they've worked their whole lives to achieve. Don't slight it, light it.

Landscape Lighting

Landscaping itself is an art form and, when properly created, is the thing that elevates the overall appearance of a home or business. Even a modest house or a small building with exceptional landscaping can look like a million bucks. Your job is to make that design shine. What looks beautiful during the day will look spectacular at night if properly lit. Be creative. Don't be afraid to try things out, add more lights, play with color and realize what shadows and effects lighting trees and shrubbery can create. Look at how the light through the trees plays on the architecture and adds wow factors. Move lights around and see what different lighting positions can create.

Perimeter lighting

Part of the job of perimeter lighting is safety. This goes double in parking areas and in places where family members can be affected. You will need to assess how to light the perimeters of the properties you're tasked to design lights for and how to balance illumination, aesthetics and safety to create an attractive, practical environment. Lighting can extend the property and gives you the opportunity to create a full and comprehensive design. Don't leave this out of the plan. They may not know they want this or need this, so tell them. Make them want every nook and cranny, every tree, fence and bush to be lit. Make them feel like this is a sexy addition to their home, office or building.

First and foremost, remember that using superior products means superior results. Know your product offering. What do I mean? Know what each fixture can do for you, how it works, what its best application is, wattage, optics.

Every component produced at Garden Light LED is made with the highest quality materials and built according to UL or ETL standards to ensure superior performance. Our lights are the Ferrari's of the industry; high-quality, sexy and built to last. We are recognized for being very visually appealing and incredibly durable. We use the best corrosion-proof CNC and milled brass, copper and stainless-steel fixtures and wire. Every component is designed to work seamlessly together under the harshest conditions. LED outdoor lighting is constantly exposed to the elements. If you want to offer equipment that can stand up to it, we know we're your best bet.

High-quality materials

Our fixtures will take on a rich patina over time, blending into any landscape design you can create and adding a beautiful decorative element. Inside those fixtures we use the most advanced LED technology, to ensure that you're selling the most elegant fixtures available that are the most efficient and reliable as well. You can offer our fixtures with pride and the knowledge that your customers are going to love you for installing them. Year after year, those fixtures will last and continue to hold their looks and value.

What makes us different?

Most other lighting companies import their products, both fixtures and electronics, while ours are built here in the U.S. Even our electrical components are made stateside and are reliable.

Our fixtures give off consistent and powerful true light output, unlike the competitors that leak and flicker. When we say, "a fixture for life," we also mean one that is adaptable to the future and is environmentally-conscious.

Maybe the best way to explain us is that we are truly American. Not only in that we build things here but that our company culture is American. Maybe if you had to light us you would use Red, White, and Blue. We think like American entrepreneurs and we build American products and other new American businesses.

The Best Warranty

Even the highest quality and best designed technology can go wrong sometimes. That's why Garden Light LED offers one of the best warranties in the industry. Our transformers and fixtures all have a lifetime warranty and our high-performance LEDs carry a 20-year warranty. No one else does that. It's unheard of. How much easier does that make your life? Do you want customers calling you at midnight to complain that their lights when out in a storm? Heck no, you don't. We don't want you calling us about it either. We did that in 2009-2010 when we were trying to bring our LED technology to the market. On top of that, they are field serviceable and easy to work on. You don't have to rip out the entire fixture and send it back to us. They're color coded. Drivers come in six different colors. We have four different light engines and four different optics. Servicing the fixtures is as easy as changing a light bulb.

Types of Lighting

Here are some types of lighting to consider when creating an Outdoor LED Lighting Design:

Decorative Lighting

A flower garden creates an alluring atmosphere during the day, but without decorative lighting at night, the backyard can become a dark black abyss. To prevent this from happening, we suggest adding lights such as the Visionary 3 (V3) LED Spotlight that will highlight the plants and give shape to the landscape.

Moonlighting Landscapes

Having bright fluorescent lights on the patio may be ideal for areas where tasks are being completed, such as cooking or reading, but they are less ideal for creating a relaxing atmosphere. That is where moonlighting prevails. This type of light comes from hanging fixtures in trees and allowing the light to cascade down on the patio. Since shadows from tree branches can be seen throughout the patio, it gives the illusion that the light source is coming from the moon. The fixtures we offer that are best suited to accomplish this is our Visionary 3 (V3) Down Light. This fixture is made specifically to hang upside down or sideways, has an internal driver and is completely sealed. Another fun thing to do is to take our Micro Max series and place them in the tree spaced out to create what looks like stars and illuminated beams of light shining down on you.

Wall Wash Lighting

This is a soft illumination effect designed to accent the texture of a wall or solid surface. For this kind of lighting we recommend our Wall Washer light which we have in large or small. Great for low lying shrubs, layering lighting, walls of course, signage, community property entrances, fences and anyplace where you need a light that may need a riser. The intention is a full, evenly distributed wash across a whole wall. I like to also use our Super Saturn Series for these effects. The Saturn's come in a single (S1) or triple light (S3) engine as well as the halo which is basically the S1 with an internal driver. It's so micro that you can install it anywhere and it throws off an insane amount of light.

Area Lighting

This type of lighting is used to illuminate a large area, such as an entire yard, without accentuating any one specific feature. This is important for families that utilize a large backyard for kids or pets or for businesses that need a well-lit parking lot area. In this case, use the Visionary 3 (V3) or the good old retrofit PVC Well Light with an S2 rather than the old-fashioned Par 36 Bulb. Path Lights are also excellent area lights.

Pathway Lighting

The most common type of lighting for a landscape is pathway lighting. This is because it not only creates a functional and safe path for a walker, but also creates visual interest within the yard. When it comes to implementing this style, it's best to stagger the lights and ensure that any obstacles or turns in the path are well illuminated. You want the light to highlight the path, not make it the focal point of the landscape. By using our stainless steel, stainless aluminum and solid brass CNC fixtures you avoid the awful problem of tipping. There's nothing worse than looking down a pathway and seeing a bunch of lights tipping and falling out of the ground. We don't let that happen.

A great style of light to achieve the perfect pathway lighting is the P12 Path Light. We have a full line of P Series Pathlight fixtures that are modern, contemporary and sleek. They put out tons of light and don't tip, God love 'em!

Spotlight Grazing

Showcasing a texture of a wall, plant or tree is one of the commonly missed opportunities when it comes to lighting. If you want to showcase a texture, whether this be a wall or a tree, then graze lighting is your best option. This form of spot light is installed close to the bottom of a straight surface with the light pointing vertically to showcase the texture. This is a great example of what I mean when I say play around with the lights and get to know them. The designer that comes in and shows a potential client what spotlight grazing can do will win that customer over. It shows a deeper level of thinking regarding design. The best lamps to use to create this effect V3, Well Lights, Mini Well Lights, The Saturn Series, S1s and S3s.

> What looks beautiful during the day will look spectacular at night if properly lit.

Up Lighting Effects

This is your sweet spot, like the comforter on the bed. The rest are just pillows. Everything is up lighting and you can use tons of it. You need to illuminate everything from the ground up. Make it look bigger and bolder. When done right, this can look incredibly striking. If done improperly, however, it will make the property look eerie. This lighting technique is known to be difficult to integrate in the landscape since it doesn't replicate a natural lighting source. That's why it's best to be aware of how the dramatic lighting effect will produce shadows.

By placing ground-level lights so they point directly up, you can create dramatic effects that highlight architectural or landscape features. Up lighting can be great for high-profile businesses like restaurants, hotels, wedding or event facilities and nightclubs. They add real drama to the look of the property and create excitement especially when color is added into the mix. Remember the 2-dimensional, 3-dimensional, and 4-dimensional lighting effect. More lights=more money. The best lamps to use to create this effect V2 and V3, Spot Lights, Well Lights, Mini Well Lights, The Saturn Series, S1s and S3s.

Deck Lighting

In addition to having lights illuminate a path, it's also important to provide adequate light sources on the deck itself. You want to ensure that the deck has lights on each stair, along the railing, and overhead lights to make the space functional well into the night. You don't want grandma or one of your guests tripping over the light fixtures and it's very important that these spaces are well-lit for safety. We usually put a longer lead wire on these fixtures, 18 gauge, that's easy to work with, because you can conceal it. Garden Light LED has a ton of fixtures for these applications. We have the Deck Light, the Deck Light Curve, the small and large Deck Light and the Pool Cage Light which fits perfectly on lanais.

Down lighting

This style of lighting is one of the more popular types since it mimics the way that natural outdoor light is created. A spotlight is hung above the ground and pointed downwards towards an object or area. The object then becomes highlighted and easily integrated into the landscape design. Some of the most common ways downlighting is used is to highlight a wall fountain, hanging flower basket or to light a path under a pergola or arbor. There are all kinds of lighting effects that you can achieve from the softness of moonlight to the bright yellow feel of the sun. Color and intensity are the major factors. Make sure you are using a completely sealed fixture for this application such as the V3 Down Light.

Docks, Fountain, Pool and Water Lighting

When lighting the pool itself, by placing fixtures underwater, you can add general illumination to a feature, or you can highlight specific objects beneath the surface. Clients love underwater lighting in pools. It enhances the nighttime swimming experience greatly and extends pool time. You can remind them how fantastic it will be to come home after a long, tough day at work and enjoy a relaxing, even romantic swim in their beautifully lit pool. It's a great selling point and yet another surface area you can add to the whole package.

One of the best lights for water, pond and pool areas is our S3 Submersible fixture which is IP-68 rated and designed and recommended specifically to go in water. Our Micro Max Series is also great for docks, decks, pool coping and pools. We sell a lot of color for these applications. Customers will want their fountains, docks, pools and ponds to be colorful. Fish love it and people love fish. Whatever you do, don't use the brass fixtures near fish. It will kill them, dead. Not good for the kiddies to see.

Spot Lighting

This type of lighting is used to illuminate a specific object, such as a statue, flag, fountain or other architectural features. Many businesses will want their American flag lit at all times. Of course, spot lighting is great for individual trees and can really enhance a long driveway that features such landscape. Spotlighting is used in so many applications, especially when lighting businesses. Spotlights can highlight the name of the business, their logo or any key architectural elements they may have on their buildings. If they like gargoyles sitting on the ledges of the building, why not light those guys? Use V2 or V3's for this job.

Shadowing

This is when a light is placed so that a tree, fountain or other element casts an interesting pattern or shadow against a wall, creating a new visual focal point. This can be very effective in creating a dynamic visual for businesses. When placed properly, this lighting can add tremendous visual effect to an otherwise dull, blank wall. All it takes is well thought out lighting. Shadow is all about cause and effect. This can be one of your greatest attributes in lighting design. The more experienced you become, the more you become adept at this kind of lighting. It can set you apart from your competitors when you get really good at manipulating these effects. V2 and V3, Well Lights, Mini Well Lights, The Saturn Series, S1s and S3s and Large and Small Wall Washers are great for this.

Silhouetting

This term refers to using back-lighting to more effectively show off an object or architectural detail. This kind of lighting is for very high dramatic effect. It can also produce an eerie effect so be careful in how you choose to use this concept. V2 and V3, Well Lights, Mini Well Lights, The Saturn Series, S1s and S3s and Large and Small Wall Washers are great for this as well.

Lighting for the Hospitality Industry

You may have been working mainly in the residential market, but you are missing great opportunities if you don't get into the hospitality market. From large hotels to small bed-and-breakfasts, the success of the business depends on attracting guests to the property, making them feel welcome, and providing them with a safe and comfortable place to stay. But it's more than just the simple things that need to be addressed and this is business you're going to want, trust me. It's big business and very lucrative.

Outdoor lighting is a crucial part of branding a hotel or restaurant. It's things like walkway lighting that guides guests safely and easily to the amenities of a hotel property; the pool, the restaurant, the outdoor bar. It's the colors you choose for that quaint Bed and Breakfast, the way you light the shrubbery and porches. It starts with choosing the right LED technology and fixtures. Garden Light Certified Master Dealers learn to handle everything from design to installation to ongoing maintenance, which gives them the edge in this market. The hospitality industry is big business and we want our installers to capture that revenue. Don't be afraid to go after these clients. When you work with us, we will guide you on how to grab this brass ring.

Worry-free maintenance

A quality LED lighting system is an investment that needs to be protected. It is the responsibility of the end-user to be sure they choose a certified and professionally trained LED company like one of our Master Dealers. Once they've signed up and have that awesome lighting design in place, we want them to stay customers for life. To that end, it's important to offer a service plan. LED systems are sensitive and absolutely need to be maintained annually. Your customers need a comprehensive service plan, so they can rest assured the warranty will be honored. As the installer, it's your responsibility to offer that service plan and explain the benefits and warn them of the issues that can ensue if the lighting system is not properly maintained. It's an opportunity to make continued money, keep the customers happy because their lights are maintained and beautiful while keeping you top of their minds for future work and referrals. Maintain their lights and the relationship with them.

We love to work with our installer partners to continue to educate and motivate them to learn more and more about lighting design. We learn from them as well. They are out in the field and they know what new innovations need to happen. The more you work as a lighting designer, the more you learn about what works and what doesn't. When one of our installer partners comes to us with an idea for a new kind of fixture, it's exciting to come up with something new and creative right in our own factory here in America.

By the way, we opted not to put pictures in this book as it would not do them justice. We have a huge gallery of our work on our website at www.gardenlightled.com/gallery if you want to check them out.

Chapter 12

Color Branding

The Psychology of Colors in Marketing

Unless you are color blind, you're are deeply affected by colors in one way or another. Have you ever seen one of those videos where a color-blind man gets a set of those new glasses that allow color blind people to see colors for the first time? Yes, it's almost always men because about 7% of men are color-blind compared to about 0.4% of women. That means for every color-blind woman there are about 17 color blind men. Something you may want to remember, chances are you won't deal with too many women who don't see color.

Color appeals greatly to our visual senses and has been a tool utilized in thousands of major brands to influence their target market. Countless studies have found that particular colors have their own effects on the consumer. Colors stimulate areas of the brain in ways which will either promote excitement or tranquility. This is important to consider when lighting areas of a person's home or if you have to light a high-energy business atmosphere.

Every light has a different color hue and light will look different on different surfaces. Not every building you light will be a blank white canvas; in fact, most won't. The use of color is something to be studied.

Primary Colors: Red, yellow and blue

Primary colors are the three pigment colors that cannot be mixed or formed by any combination of other colors. *All* other colors are derived from these three hues. That's pretty interesting when you really think about it.

Color in lighting is different than color in paint. If pure red, blue, and yellow paints are mixed together, the result will be black. When mixing light, the opposite effect happens. If you shine pure red, blue, and yellow light on a wall, you will get white.

Secondary Colors: Green, orange and purple

These are the colors formed by mixing the primary colors.

Tertiary Colors: Yellow-orange, red-orange, red-purple, blue-purple, blue-green & yellow-green

These are the colors formed by mixing a primary and a secondary color. That's why the hue is a two-word name, such as blue-green, red-violet, and yellow-orange.

Choosing colors in lighting, like with paint, is both an art and a science. You have to find the colors that work together best to achieve the results you're looking for. If you can position yourself as a color expert, not only can you create great designs for residential properties, but you can help businesses establish their brand through the use of color.

Color Harmony

Whether it's music, poetry, cooking, or color, harmony means a sense of order, a balance in the visual experience. Remember that the opposite of harmony is chaos. When you're creating a lighting design, you need to balance the colors so there is harmony. Too many colors, especially ones that don't work well together, can create a visual experience that's overdone and over stimulating to the brain. The human brain rejects what it cannot organize or understand.

The human brain also will reject under-stimulating information. In other words, if the colors are dull, the human brain rejects them as boring. Color harmony delivers visual interest and a sense of order.

Let's look at the way some colors can influence people.

Some statistics:

- 84.7% of buyers claim color is the primary draw to a product.
- 52% of customers won't return to a store if they dislike the aesthetic.
- 80% of clients believe colors are responsible for brand recognition.

Some specifics about colors:

Red

Red can encourage appetite, so it's often used by fast-food chains and food products. McDonalds and Coke are two of the biggest brands in the world and both use a deep red.

Red is often associated with movement, passion, and excitement. We all know that red is the color of Valentine hearts and candy boxes. We've created a whole romantic theme around red roses and hearts. Red is fiery and passionate.

Red also exudes high energy and immediately pulls ones focus toward it. Using red lighting, when appropriate, could draw the eye of the consumer toward the object being lit.

It physically stimulates the human body, affecting nerve impulses, raising blood pressure and heart rate.

Red is a great color to use when seeking to grab attention, get a reaction, perhaps evoke passion or even romance. If your client wants to stir up action and excitement, red is a good choice for lighting.

Red can also be perceived as angry or even violent. It depends on the depth of the color and the usage and intensity.

Considering all of that, red is a great choice for a lighting design that offers the client a high-energy, wow, in-your-face experience if brightly and fully lit. Softer red lighting can mean romance and passion. Use red wisely and appropriately.

Blue

Not surprisingly, blue is preferred by men. We associate blue with boys and pink with girls. Centuries ago the opposite was true. Pink was originally the color associated with boys and blue with girls, but that has changed and has really stuck. If you want to appeal to men, pink lighting will probably not be the way to go, but it would be great for a women's boutique or when trying to attract a highly-feminine audience.

Blue, however, attracts male centric audiences, partly because they have been surrounded by that color since birth with their blankets and clothing.

Young people associate blue with maturity. Lots of hospitals and medical offices utilize blue. It has the effect of calming the mind, providing a sense of tranquility and space and creates a sense of security.

Blue is the color of water and the sky. When lighting someone's home, blue is a good choice for areas where the family will want to enjoy some peaceful moments.

On the downside, blue can be associated with sadness. We all know the expression, "having the blues." Be cautious not to use blue in a way that feels depressing.

Green

Green is most associated with health, tranquility and nature. When lighting trees and foliage, even though they are already green, you may consider using green lighting to enhance their natural beauty.

Green is also closely associated with money and wealthy people or brands. This is something to consider when lighting a business that may want to elicit the response from customers that this business will bring them wealth. Show them the green and show them the money.

It can also be used to relax customers, so green can be a great choice for residential lighting and around businesses that want people to feel comfortable and at home.

Green stimulates harmony in the brain and encourages balance between body and emotion, leading to decisiveness as well.

Purple

Purple is often associated with royalty, wisdom and respect. If someone wants their home to feel majestic, purple might appeal to them. Imagine up-lighting a three-story home with purple lighting. To some people, that might feel like they are coming home to a castle.

Purple stimulates the problem-solving area of the brain as well as creativity. It's a great choice for areas where kids and teens might frequent. Playgrounds, community centers and art facilities are great choices for the use of the color purple.

In marketing, purple is frequently used for beauty and anti-aging products and represents a creative, wise and imaginative brand. Keep that in mind for your commercial projects that might be well-suited to the use of this color.

Orange and Yellow

These two colors are most closely related to the increase in cheerfulness and optimism.

They're often used to draw in impulsive buyers and window shoppers and they stimulate the logic center of the brain and promote enthusiasm.

Choosing brighter colors leads to people feeling more energetic and, as a result, can better evoke response or reaction from them.

Whether it's music, poetry, cooking, or color, harmony means a sense of order, a balance in the visual experience.

These two colors are also very kid-friendly, so make use of these colors when tasked to deal with areas that young kids will be engaging with.

Color effects people's perception in profound ways. In Scotland in the year 2000, the city of Glasgow installed blue street lighting in some of their neighborhoods and reported reduced crime in those areas. Not that you want to promise clients that blue will keep crime down in their neighborhood, but that's something to note for sure.

A railroad company in Japan installed blue lighting at its stations in 2009 in an effort to reduce the number of suicide attempts, though it wasn't proven to work. Still, if the Japanese gave it a shot, you know they did some research. They have a very high suicide rate there. It would be interesting to find out if this technique was helping with that.

Color preference may depend on ambient temperature. People who live in colder climates seem to prefer warm colors like red and yellow while people who reside in hotter climates are likely to prefer cool colors like blue and green. Red and Yellow lighting can literally trick the mind into believing the air is warmer and the reverse with blue and green lighting. Color is that powerful.

Color Theory

Color Theory actually covers a number of things, but at the most basic level it is the interaction of colors in a design through complementation, contrast and vibrancy.

Complementation

This refers to the way we see colors in terms of their relationships with other colors. When colors from opposite ends of the spectrum are paired together, viewers consider them more appealing. They are called "complementary colors" because the eye sees this as balance through the combination of these two opposites. Complementation can take you to new levels of design sophistication when you can begin to master the intricacies of color combinations. This kind of understanding and knowledge comes with time in the field, practicing and experimenting on your own, and studying color wheels and charts. If you take the time to get to know what colors working together can create visually and emotionally, you will be so far ahead of the competition they won't be able to see you.

Contrast

Refers to a clear division of elements in a design, which reduces eyestrain and allows the viewer to focus their attention. Be conscious of how you choose colors for your background objects, like walls and other large sections of architecture and the objects in the landscape like trees, bushes, arbors or fencing can create contrast. If you are ever in doubt, the rule of thumb is use a lighter color for the background and a darker color for the objects that surround it.

Vibrancy

Not to get all woo-woo, but vibrancy is what dictates the *emotion* of your design. Brighter colors create a more energetic result for your design, which is particularly effective when you're trying get an emotional response. Darker shades are relaxing, allowing people's minds to focus on other things. Color choices, brightness and color blending can elicit strong emotions. You're the one making those decisions with the client. It's psychology and you have to study it and get to know the people whose property you're being entrusted to light. In a way, you have a piece of their lives in your hands.

The beauty of where we are in history right now is that we can benefit from centuries of scientific and artistic color theorists. There are entire volumes that have been written about the minutia of color theory. There's so much material you can get, so much information on the web and in books and in videos on YouTube, you have to take the time and make the effort. It's your money, your bottom line that will be affected. The more you know the more sought after you'll be.

Potential Color Branding Clients

What kind of clients are very concerned about color branding? Where can you pitch the fact that you are an expert at color blending and color theory in lighting?

Here are some ideas on that.

Independent manufacturer reps – they have clients that are looking for you and will be seeking your expertise.

Advertising and branding agencies – look up local marketing companies that specialize in branding and tell them about your company and what you can do for their commercial clients; how you can light their facilities and assist in color branding.

Architectural firms & hotel management companies – They need you and your expertise in color theory and branding. We actually work with a hotel chain (can't tell you which one, sorry) that we have helped create their own color branding. It sets them apart completely. When you pull up to a hotel and you can recognize which brand name chain it's part of, just by the color of the lighting on the property, that's color branding my friends. That's what McDonalds offers. You can see McDonalds from blocks away or off the road on a highway and you know there is an Egg McMuffin in your future. They get branding.

Corporate Headquarters and Franchises – Big money here. Branding is everything with them. Latch on to a new franchise or one that is considering a rebranding and let them know you can create lighting that will increase their brand awareness and they will fight to hire you.

Local Businesses – Every local business needs lighting. Let them know you are an expert on color theory and lighting and that you can enhance their brand and attract clients with great lighting.

Reach out to businesses such as:

- Hotels
- Bars
- Restaurants
- Yoga studio's

- Gym's
- Banks
- Colleges and Universities
- Churches
- Sports arenas
- Concert or performing art centers
- Resorts and Spa's
- Golf Courses and Country Clubs
- City Walks and Airports
- CEOs, Doctors, Lawyers

They all need lighting and they all have some sort of branding in place or need to have new branding. Lighting their building and grounds to be consistent with that branding or helping them utilize lighting in their branding is essential for them. If they don't realize that, educate them. Do a lighting demo and show them how you can enhance their brand; take it to a new level.

If you learn all you can about color and take the time to reach out to people that will want your level of expertise, you can dominate in your market area and make yourself and your company a sought-after commodity. It's another step toward the million-dollar business we want you to create.

Chapter 13

Installation

As a lighting designer, you are creating value and innovation in the world. LED lighting is a beautiful concept; however, it needs to be well designed, properly installed, and regularly serviced.

When it comes down to it, you are the most important component just like a chef is the most important component in creating a gourmet meal. Two different cooks, with the same ingredients, the same kitchen to work in, the same equipment, will make two entirely different dishes. Just watch a few episodes of Chopped if you don't believe me. Embrace this concept and enjoy it. Be the chef!

At Garden Light LED, all of our Master Dealers and Installers are rigorously trained and certified, both in the classroom and in the field. They are taught the best practices that we have developed over our years of manufacturing experience. Our installers learn to bring expert knowledge, creativity and meticulous attention to detail to every single installation. They know that they must treat every property, and every installation, as a unique project, not just a scripted appointment. The goal is to produce outstanding results the first time, every time.

It's critical that installers arrive on time, when promised, and leave the customer's property in the same or better condition than when they arrived. We often hear from customers that they have never encountered the level of professionalism in a service provider before, and that is a benchmark we continually try to achieve at Garden Light LED. It's what we want every one of our Master Dealers to achieve at all times.

Lighting Designers want to design, not install. We get it. They learned this art form in a school that probably cost them a lot of money to attend. The idea of getting on the ground and running wires isn't appealing to them. It may not be to you either, but if you're accepted into our Master Dealer Program, you're going to learn to install lights. We're going to teach you the best practices, but more importantly, our installer partners are going to take you on actual job sites and you will be getting your hands dirty working with them. They do this every day and they are the pros. It's a crash course in installing lights and, like most on the job training, it's the best and quickest way to learn.

Here are some technical instructions that you will need to learn as an installer:

Halogen, LED & Transformer Installation Instructions:

Halogen Installation

In a Halogen System, make sure that the distance between the first and last fixture in a single run is no longer than 30 ft. for 12/2 wire and no longer than 45 ft. for 10/2.

- You will lose 1 Volt for every 50 feet away from the transformer.
- The farther you travel from the transformer, the more resistance you will have on a run.

Most halogen applications will use 10/2 wire.

Recommendation: Use 10/2 wire on longer runs with more wattage. With 10/2 wire, you will have less wire resistance. It holds more wattage because it has more strands of copper.

- Please review installation sheets provided with each fixture

LED Installation

When installing LED fixtures, make sure that the distance between the transformer and last fixture in a single run is no longer than 200 ft. for 12/2 wire. Most LED applications will use 12/2 wire. For distances longer than 200 ft., please call your Territory Manager.

Use 10/2 wire on longer runs with more wattage, with 10/2 wire you will have less wire resistance. It holds more wattage because it has more strands of copper.

Please consult your Expert LED Consultant for assistance in selecting Wire or Transformer Size.

LED Transformer Installation

Primary

- Consists of the transformer, photocell and timer

120 volts out of the outlet. Use a volt meter to calculate exactly what your reading is (could be 110-125, this will

affect the output in the secondary). You can perform additional checks; however, it is not mandatory.

- Check the voltage at each tap and check the amperage at the photocell loop (it should read no more than .01-.03). There are transformers built by other manufacturers with higher readings. A higher reading will indicate that you already have used up some of the wattage on your transformer.

Fixture selection – Attending tactical dealer congress events are a priority. Knowing your product and the intricate things you can achieve with a great lighting design is the essence of your success. Utilizing the LED lighting fixtures to create a total lighting design no other lighting company or lighting designer ever thought about is key. The difference is having your hands on the ground and experimenting with the LED lighting products.

Keep your selections limited, yet precise. Design is design, no matter what the application. Think of this analogy: a bullet light application is the comforter on the bed and the accent lights, such as well lights, mini well lights, X-lights, path lights and micro max are the pillows. Together they create a balanced look. Create lighting effects with different light output, fixtures, optics and colors.

Transformer selection – Use a 12 Volt transformer that is UL listed and Made in the USA. Multi-tap and magnetic breakers. Be sure that transformers are LED transformers with surge protection on the primary and the secondary. GLLED's transformers are unparalleled and offer all of these features.

Controls and Dimming – This is the future of lighting. Our LED lights can be dimmed. Many people will want this feature in their LED lighting system. Be able to offer it. Our fixtures are compatible with Lutron and Crestron drivers.

Wire calculation – Be sure to use Marine grade wire. Add the wattage of each fixture on the run.

Core-drilling – It is very important that you use a diamond tipped core bit 1 1/2 inch for drilling mini well Lights. Before you begin drilling, you must make a template with a quarter inch piece of plywood just large enough to put your feet on either side of and hold it as a brace so you do not damage the surface of the stone or tile when you try to start your initial drilling.

Just pre-drill a hole in the plywood in the grass or dirt and your template will be ready. Keep in mind how far your holes are away from the wall and keep them all the same distance so that you achieve the same illumination. Make sure, as you're core drilling, to slightly waller the hole, moving the drill bit left to right as you're drilling to keep the drill from binding and getting stuck. Also make sure you drill the hole all the way through the concrete surface and expose the dirt as it allows for the water to perk out of the light hole.

Concealing wire – Always pre-drill all of your holes before you start cutting grout joints for wiring, as you can get a better idea of what joints to cut. Use a diamond-tipped 7-inch Makita blade on a grinder wheel for cutting grout joints or mortar joints. Only open the joint the thickness of the sawblade and go deep enough to fully bury two wires deeply where you cannot see them before the grout goes back in. Once you have all your grout joints cut, use 14 stranded wire to roll it right in the joints. Push it deep enough in the light hole so if you ever have to pull right out, the wire comes out far enough to re-crimp connections. Chip out an old section of grout to expose the body of the grout, which will be the original color. Generally, the top surface will be dirty with sediment. Once you grout the surface, you may need to apply a little dirt on top of it to match the existing grout. Just muddy it up a little bit.

When it comes down to it, you are the most important component just like a chef is the most important component in creating a gourmet meal.

Matching stucco and finishes – When matching stucco surfaces, always used an approved stucco sponge float. It will be green. Bring out the proper aggregate on the sand finish stucco job by very gently applying, using virtually no pressure, with a damp, but not soaking wet, sponge. Gently wipe in a circular motion to achieve a good match, making sure to spread out from the actual joint at least several inches.

You must understand that these are low-voltage plug and play lighting systems. You don't need to be an electrician to own a LED lighting business.

When voltage at the beginning of a length of cable (at the transformer) is higher than the voltage at the end, the difference is known as "voltage drop". The visual indicator of voltage drop is dim light fixtures at the end of a cable run. The closer the light fixtures are to the transformer, the higher the voltage and brightness. Voltage drop can be minimized through proper selection of the cable size based on total wattage load and the length of run. This "wizard" will help you determine the proper wire size and transformer to maximize light output with minimum voltage drop, while also protecting the bulbs from premature burnout.

There is an app we recommend you download - **Landscape Lighting Calculator.** It calculates wires, runs and wattage for you.

When you install our lighting fixtures the way we teach you to install, you are doing a 20-year installation. Our fixtures carry a 20-year guarantee and the transformer we use, our wiring and equipment, when installed our way, make the system built to last. LED fixtures are sensitive to heat and humidity. They aren't built to last. Our fixtures are 40% cooler with surge protectors on all fixtures. There are surge protectors on our transformers primary and secondary. All of our equipment is specifically made for LED with arching and heat and humidity prevention.

This is the most important part of what you do, Garden Light LED systems will run a lifetime if installed properly. 80% of the time, failure is due to improper installation.

You will use non-corrosive Marine grade wire on your installs. Every single copper strand inside the wiring is coated with plastic coating. This prevents arching 100% of the time. We recommend using a holistic system for LED lighting systems.

Tools you will need include:

Mallet
Shovel

Ladder
Knee pads
Crimpers
Wire cutters/stripers
Electrical tape
PVC – ½" and 3/4'"
Stainless Steel Screws – Only use stainless screws for exterior.
Phillips screw driver - assorted sizes
Flathead screw driver – various sizes
Hammer drill screw gun
Makita grinder – with a diamond blade (for cutting grout joints).
1 ½" Diamond Core bit – various sizes

Shoveling – Use your foot gently and create a small trench, also avoid digging deeply and damaging the landscape or cutting into wires.

LED Transformer – ALWAYS use the 15-tap when wiring a LED lighting system to ensure the last light on the run is getting the same amount of power. Exception, if hooking one or two lights only or run is close to the house, then use 12-tap.

When wiring the transformer, lay the transformer on the ground to ensure you can see what you are doing. Get the wire deep enough to ensure the wire doesn't burn and damage the transformer or the lights.

Mounting the transformer – On the wall, only use stainless steel screws. Do not use tapcon as they will rust and look terrible.

Transformer triple protection LED – Wire the LED Protection Kit into the system with one lead in the 15v Tap, and the second on the Common Tap. The most vulnerable part of the Lighting System is the Fixture's Driver and adding an additional layer of protection prolongs the life of the system, adding value to the end user.

Photocell – This plugs into the transformer and needs to be around a little bit of light. When the sun goes down, it causes the system to go on. When the sun comes up, the lights go off.

Timer – Digital or analog Astronomical timer – sets your system to whatever off and on times you prefer.

Wire – Only use noncorrosive Marine grade wire – you have an option to use conduit to install the system, however it is not a requirement and would be considered an upgrade. I do recommend using conduit from transform to the ground and anywhere the beds or landscape goes to grass.

We recommend barring the wire 2 inches, unless near a root system, then it is recommended you bury the wire one inch.

Gas tight drum connectors – Feed the unconnected wires though the wire slots of the connector. Join wires together, then insert into grease-filled capsule to prevent water intrusion.

Calculating wattage – Step one, before anything calculate the wattage of each fixture.

It is very important that you do not exceed wattage on one line.

Basic rule, most of your lighting systems will be installed with 12/2.

Wiring the system

100 watts per run – 12/2 200 ft. and under from the transformer

180 watts per run – 10/2 any runs over 200 ft.

Once you have calculated the total wattage of the fixtures, move onto light placement and determine the number of runs necessary. I always recommend drawing a diagram of the project plan to reference when servicing and repairing the lighting systems.

Stake installation – Use the mallet. It's very important to make sure the stake is fully inserted in the ground.

Strategic Partners

"**S**tand on the shoulders of giants." There are people that have been in this business for years and it may surprise you to know that many, if not most of them, are happy to share information with you. It feels good to be an expert, and it does them no harm to help you. You can stand on their shoulders. Some of them will be partners and some will be mentors. Don't be afraid to reach out to them. All of our Master Dealers understand this, and we will explain in detail in our final chapter how our veteran installers work with the folks in our Master Dealer program.

But there are also people who you will be shoulder to shoulder with; businesses who touch up against what you do. They will find a relationship with you to be as beneficial to them as it is to you.

At Garden Light LED we live by the concept that connections are everything. No one can run a highly-successful business without creating and nurturing strong connections to strategic partners. This is takes time and commitment to make it a reality, but it is an absolute must.

So, who are these people you need to partner with? Let's consider them.

Architects & Specifiers

Architects would be wise to meet with lighting design professionals when they are drawing up plans for a new home or rebuild. Anyone that is hiring an architect to design their project is taking that project seriously. Why would they not consider how they're going to light it?

Specifiers are the guys who determine the scope of a project. As for what in their job description pertains to our business, they calculate optics wattage and do all the dirty work regarding the electrical needs of the structure being built. Be nice to them. You want them on your side.

Other Lighting designers and Installers

Most lighting designers hate installing and therefore do not do it. They don't like to get their hands dirty. They went to school to be lighting designers, but no one told them how to hook the suckers up. When you get into our Master Dealer Program, we are going to teach you to be an installer. You're going to have on the job training with one of our master installers to learn the proper methods for installation and reduce any trepidation you might have about it. You'll learn how to become a master of lighting design as well. So, it behooves you to partner with, get to know, and become friendly with other lighting designers and installers. You'll learn from them, share information with them, and sometimes hand off work to them or do work for them. They're your colleagues. Some may become mentors, and as you grow, you may mentor others down the line. Maybe you will find you have a knack for something some of the other designers and installers aren't as adept at. Be their go-to person for that niche.

Electricians

It's not unlikely that you will need to call on electricians from time to time. Once you establish a camaraderie with some of them, they will be there to make you look good and they will think of you when a client calls them to refer a lighting design professional.

Landscapers: These guys really need you. What is the point of spending a ton of money on beautiful landscaping to only be able to see it in daylight? Get with them and create a relationship. You should be able to recommend each other and partner on projects often.

Paver companies: Again, a beautiful driveway, walkway or patio that isn't lit? Foolish. Get with these guys. They're money in the bank.

Pool companies: You have the special tools to properly light a pool. When you work with us, we can offer you great underwater lighting. Of course, the pool area will need to be lit as well. No pool company should offer to put in a pool without having a go-to lighting company they can rely on.

Contractors: Find the people in your area that build big houses and/or commercial build outs. Considering the lighting when building makes sense. Why wait till the home or office building is up to figure out where the lighting will go? Get cozy with contractors. They're big money.

Interior Designers: These folks tend to build strong relationships with their customers. They can be great referral partners if you impress them. They will only recommend a company they truly know, like, and trust to their clients.

Outdoor furniture companies – Outdoor living is the new big thing. The furniture people put outside these days is nicer than the furniture we had in our home when I was a kid. We work and live in Florida, where we have great weather for outdoor enjoyment a lot of the year. Trust me, you want to get to know these guys and be able to work together. Even in colder climates, people love their outdoor activities. Light up their outdoor world.

Outdoor kitchen companies: Outdoor kitchens are all the rage and not cheap to set up. Contact the people that install them and see how you might enhance these amazing set-ups with awesome lighting.

Fencing companies: Safety is a big reason for fencing in a property. Keep kids and dogs in and intruders out. Light those fences. These guys really need to connect with you.

Audio Visual companies – Companies that offer Smart Home Integration - Google home programmers need to talk with you about garage doors, security lights and all kinds of dimmable elements. Our lights can be dimmed, and they are Crestron and Lutron certified so they work with those dimmers. The company Lutron was started in 1959 by Joel S. Spira. In 1961, he invented a dimmer based on a diode and a tapped autotransformer, thus saving energy and allowing the dimmer to be installed in a standard electrical wall box. His dimmer is the control component of the power supply that allows lights to be dimmed and we still use it today.

Manufacturer Reps – These distributors carry lots of products and lines. They want to sell those products. Without you, they have no business. Manufacturer reps have been around for decades. They are an extended sales force for businesses without the overhead. However, you are the value innovation they need to sell, design and install lighting systems. When creating relationships with these companies, look for reps that are innovative and seek real-time money-making opportunities. The high-end spec market needs the design, install and service solution. They are not aware it exists. Manufacturer reps are in every major market throughout the United States. The largest and publicly-traded companies have reps strategically located to drive sales in the high-end spec market worldwide. Have you driven by hotel franchises and restaurants and thought, I would love to show these companies a proper lighting system? The manufacturer reps are your way into those locations. Without them, chances are you may not break into these bigger companies.

_____

Build an army.

_____

Be aware of these five players listed below. They are the big dogs in the field and have a wealth of knowledge. It's important to look at the landscape and know what's out there.

Acuity – Acuity Brands, Inc. (NYSE: AYI) is the North American market leader and one of the world's leading providers of lighting and building management solutions for commercial, institutional, industrial, infrastructure and residential applications throughout North America and select international markets. Acuity Brands currently employs over 12,000 associates and is headquartered in Atlanta, Georgia with operations throughout North America and in Europe and Asia.

Hubbell – Hubbell Inc. is an international manufacturer of quality electrical and electronic products for a broad range of residential and non-residential construction, industrial and utility applications. They are headquartered in Shelton, CT, and operate manufacturing facilities in the U.S. and around the world.

Eaton Cooper – Eaton is a leader in power management solutions for customers in more than 175 countries worldwide.

Phillips – Philips has been revolutionizing lighting for over 125 years. They pioneered the world-changing development of electric light and LED.

Lithonia – Lithonia Lighting, an Acuity Brands Company, has been around for more than 60 years, providing the industry's broadest line of commercial, industrial, institutional and residential fixtures. Their products are known for quality, reliability and solid performance.

Visit with these distributors. As lighting designers, you have a product and service people need to know about.

Garden Light LED – We are strategic partners for all of our installers. We want that relationship with you. Our *What* is two-fold: One - our product line; creating the best LED lighting fixtures and equipment made in America today. Two - helping build creative, successful businesses that partner with us. When you do well, we do well. We sell the best lighting fixtures available in the marketplace and we know that when our installers use our products they have an advantage over other lighting professionals. We know what kind of quality we offer and we're damn proud of it. The more of you that learn how to run and grow a successful lighting business, the more product you will buy from us because we make it easy for you. Not only do we teach you the best practices, have the best mentors for you to learn from and partner with, but our products won't fail you or your customers.

We are in the business of designing, building, and ultimately selling light fixtures and equipment. We want to sell lots of product. We want to grow our business, hire more people, innovate more, create more and be known as THE best in the business.

How can we best do that? By helping others build and grow their business and show them the value of using superior products; by creating Master Dealers who would then be our strategic partners. We're not McDonalds. We don't make you buy our napkins, burger patties and buns. The choice is yours, but most of our Master Dealers buy most of their products from us by choice, not out of loyalty to us. They just want the best for their customers.

You can build your business the same way we did and still do. Connect with others, create strategic partnerships with us and all kinds of other businesses.

Build an army.

Chapter 15

Mentorship 101

What is a mentor?

If you were lucky, like I was, you would have had the advantage of growing up with values. I was taught, at an early age that it's imperative to surround yourself with people who know more than you do; people that can help take you where you want to be.

As I was growing up, I had a great role model in my grandfather, Howard Clarence Dietzel. He was from Saginaw Michigan, my mom's dad, a man of honor and integrity, and the consummate entrepreneur. I watched and learned from him, and over his lifetime, as well as mine, he owned many businesses. He was a general contractor by trade but tried his hand at owning a golf course and a restaurant and had the guts to jump in on any opportunity that he thought had real potential. He was a millionaire more than once in his life, and more than once lost it all. But he never quit.

In 2009, already in his 80's, he decided he wanted to work with Reto and me. He was so intrigued with what we do; with lighting the world. And what a joy and a benefit to have his wisdom and ingenuity with me day by day.

He had always been my favorite person on the planet; and I, his. All my life, I knew I could go to him for loving advice. I was the apple of his eye when I was younger, and he was always there for me. I talked to him every day about everything from life, relationships, family, and business. He always listened to me and gave me his time. This was and always will be the most incredible relationship of my life.

My own dad was very principled and taught me lot, but he remarried when I was five and had a new family. He traveled a lot, so I saw little of him, but he was intelligent, disciplined and ethical. He too was a great role model, but not the constant and unwavering one that was my grandfather. My world could be crashing, but I would always be able to reach out to my grandfather and know I would not be let down.

Now, as an adult, coming into my own success, my grandfather showed up to help me build my family's business. He was such a valuable asset. We would strategize with him, and he would come back with ideas, solutions, and next steps. He helped me see the future of this business.

At nearly 90 he was still selling lighting, working with us. He took Plant City as his territory; his stomping grounds.

"I want to sell lighting in Plant City," he said.

"Go for it," I replied. "Have at it, man."

And so, he did. Even though he was pretty-darned old and getting feeble, he wanted to be vital. He still wanted in on the game. The guy was never a quitter, and that's one thing he passed on to me.

I don't do lazy.

He worked to build a relationship with the development at Stonybrook Lakes, still wheeling and dealing in his late 80s, out in Plant City where he lived.

We would like nothing more than to have you become our next success story!

He loved our business so much that he would go to appointments, oxygen tank and all.

"Hang on; I need some air." He would tell the clients, taking a puff of oxygen and continuing. They loved him; loved his zest for life and business and that, even at his age, he could get excited about work, about lighting their homes and businesses.

Finally, the last two years of his life, it became too much to continue to work, and we had to set him up in a nursing home. Howard Dietzel was as German as German can be. At the end of his life, in a nursing home in Ybor City, Florida, he was surrounded by Spanish and African American people whom he had had very little contact with over his lifetime. What a learning experience. He quickly made friends with everyone and I think it enriched his life and perhaps kept him alive a little longer. The man was adaptable, pliable, resilient, and a champ in every way possible.

We lost him in 2013 but his help was immeasurable almost until the day he died, and I will love him till the day I do.

If you're fortunate, you have had someone like that in your formative years. If not, you must learn to seek out true mentors.

Finding a million-dollar mentor:

Mentors come from different places and in different ways. One person, whom I have yet to meet, who has mentored me through her work and writing, is Janet Moyer. Reto handed me her book, The Landscape Lighting Book, 18 years ago and told me to read it and learn. He was right. The book is the manifesto on landscape lighting.

Janet Lennox Moyer studied interior design but fell in love with lighting. She worked at the Architectural Engineering firm Smith, Hinchman & Grylls in the 1970's then moved to California where for the following 20 years, she focused on landscape lighting. Very little information was available about landscape lighting at that time. After years of figuring out how to create beautiful night environments and educating herself about how to specify a fixture that will hold up in the destructive outdoor environment, Jan worked with John Wiley and Sons to produce The Landscape Lighting Book. In the 1990's Jan moved to upstate New York and in 2010 founded The Landscape Lighting Resource Center, a 501(c)3 educational public charity, sharing information about and training people interested in landscape lighting.

She creates mentoring program and events and is at the top of my wish list to speak at a future dealer congress.

Paul Gosselin is an AOLP, CLVLT, COLD Certified Technician who wrote an excellent book called, The Landscape Lighting Guide: A complete guide to building a low voltage LED landscape lighting business.

The book claims to be able to help almost anyone create a successful business in low voltage LED landscape lighting. He created a simple guide for the potential outdoor lighting entrepreneur to take people through the basic steps from choosing a company name to completing the installation of a quality outdoor lighting system. It isn't filled with a lot of technical jargon, or boring information, and you don't need a college education to understand it all.

Paul gets it. This book should be on the top of the reading list, especially for newcomers to the field.

My first real business mentor

I was fresh on the job working for the magazines and went on my first sales call. At that appointment, I met a man that became my first business mentor. He wasn't interested in advertising in the magazines, despite the fact that I truly felt he should, and did my best to convince him of that.

He argued his point, and rather than send me off without another thought he instead gave me a book, The 22 Immutable Laws of Marketing. He told me to read it and come back to him, and I did. Not only did I read it in just a couple of days, but I marked it up and had questions.

He threw a ball, and I went after it.

So, he took me seriously, and now I had his full attention. He knew I wanted to learn, and he admired that. Over the next few years, he gave me structure in my life. I knew I could go to him with problems, ideas, strategies. He had gone to the college of my dreams, Wharton School of Business. He used the pillars of success that he learned at Wharton in every aspect of his career and life. I couldn't learn fast enough. I was a sponge, and he respected that about me. That one failed sales call, my very first sales call, as a matter of fact, led to a 25-year friendship and the most valuable business mentorship anyone could hope to have.

Right place, right time? Fate? Destiny? You got me, but regardless, I know what a blessing that was.

I covet a degree from Wharton, always have, always will, and working with my mentor all those years was like getting a personal, Wharton level, education with him. He was a marketing genius who worked with five of the best-known Fortune 500 companies to build each of their entire exclusive dealer programs. He knew how to spend their money, really well. He was used to having big budgets to play with. From watching him use that money, I learned that you must have measures. We're a far smaller business with a far smaller budget. We could not and cannot spend the way he was used to.

Sometimes you learn what not to do from a mentor too.

In 2015, he and I spent over 200 hours together, working on creating the strategic plan for the company; current customers, performing inventory SKU's, current market exposure. The Pareto Principle prevailed every time, in every instance; the 80/20 rule - 80% of the effects come from 20% of the causes. We worked to create our game-changing program for our installers, utilizing the digital marketing platform for GLLED which is used in big business and many verticals. We utilized the same concepts that he had implemented in working with those fortune 500 companies. It's cutting-edge stuff and our little company latched on to it.

Another mentor

A man named Ken Nulman walked up to me at LightFair, 2017 and said, "I am in love with your product." Well, that's nice to hear from anyone, but Ken is not just anyone. He is a 4th generation lighting manufacturer and owner of Nulco Lighting, Architectural Lighting Systems (ALS) and Davis/ Muller Lighting.

Ken formed Lighting Introductions, LLC in 2013. It was always his interest to stay true to his core beliefs and to share his extensive lighting and marketing knowledge and experience, including experience learned by failures as well as by successes. Ken created Lighting Introductions to bring together unique and exemplary parties who would profit by working together. An introduction could be simply matching a sales agent with a supplier; or introducing a supplier to produce product for another and to share marketing, patents, or other assets in each other's market, or to cooperate in any way that is mutually beneficial.

Fortunately for us, he was totally overwhelmed by the quality of our products and our commitment to excellence. Ken decided that Garden Light would be his only new supplier commitment for the year and brought several prospective representatives to meet us before the end of the show.

Ken's current interest is the great potential of new technologies, particularly in the medical and food processing markets. These markets include lighting fixtures integrated with wave-length controlled LED for medical purposes, bio-sterilization, and clean room products for use in hospitals, food processing and warehouses, restaurants, cafeterias and salad bars.

Off-grid products for areas such as the Sub Sahara and areas ravaged by natural disasters excite Ken for the great humanitarian benefits they provide. He presently works with a number of partners in this area, including some of the most generous humanitarians who also provide thousands of jobs and opportunities for women in the neediest areas of the world.

Ken was born in 1940, and in 1950 at age ten, he enthusiastically committed to his father that he would enter the family lighting business. In 1962 he graduated from the University of Pennsylvania with honors in history and from there attended MIT, Sloan School of Industrial Management. But the lure of the family business, Nulco Lighting, drew him home after only one year.

Can you see why having a man of this quality, one who has literally spent his entire life working in and improving our industry, would be highly beneficial? I can't say enough about him or all he has done to help Reto and I professionally and knowing him on a personal level has been a joy.

People of the ilk of the mentors I have had the fortune to have in my life, know that the greater part of the reward for a mentor is to share his or her knowledge, successes, and failures. Knowledge is not something to horde. There are no "secrets" to hold on to. Sharing the things you have learned, the pitfalls you have navigated, the trials, errors, positives, negatives, and all the good, bad, and ugly, advances you. It's no loss to a mentor to share this information. It's to their benefit as much as it is to the mentee. Pay it forward when you are in that position, and if you do the work, you will be in that position sooner that you think.

The student will inevitably become the master.

Two other mentors I must mention.

Topher Morrison. I was fortunate to have met Topher and become part of his Key Person of Influence (KPI) program. Yes, I am still working with and seeking new mentors. My theater-minded friends remind me that Meryl Streep still attends acting classes and workshops. There is always more to learn. You're never done.

Topher's group, guided by his expert hand, is such a blessing. I continue to learn and grow with his guidance. He teaches me to be a better speaker and presenter, and it's KPI's influence and encouragement that helped me forge forward to write this book.

Kevin Harrington. Kevin is a big deal. He is a multi-millionaire, an original shark from the TV show, Shark Tank, and in reality, doesn't have to help anyone.

And yet he does.

Why? Because he is a true mentor. He knows that keeping his knowledge to himself is hiding his light under a bushel and does no one any good. I am grateful to him for the time he gives me, the wisdom he shares with me. His time is valuable and limited and yet he always makes time for me.

Do you know what it's like to know that a man like this will answer the phone when I call? I hope you will find mentors like this, especially in our industry, that will answer the phone for you. That's what our mentor program will strive to do for you; create those strategic partnerships and mentor/mentee relationships.

Reto and Michelle - The What and Why of Us.

Reto and I have been mentoring each other like a seesaw, back and forth, for our entire relationship. We're both working hard to be the kind of mentors in our kid's life that my grandfather was in mine. We are each other's what and why, and, hopefully, theirs as well. We strive to teach our four kiddos what a mentor looks like, and how to find them in other places.

And we strive to be good mentors to the people we work with. We never wanted to be just a company that builds lights. We want to be a company that builds people.

Reto is a true mentor. He loves sharing his knowledge. We knew that if we found people with the right mixture of tenacity, drive, and willingness to learn, we could teach them what we know and help them become enormous successes.

One such success story is that of Kyle McKelvy. Kyle went through rigorous mentoring with Reto and became a model mentee. Kyle is a former Air Force firefighter, who we met through his wife who, at the time, was the nanny to our children. Kyle had gone straight from high school into the military and was 21 years old when we met him.

He was intrigued by our business and wanted to try something new and exciting. Reto promised him that if he followed our step-by-step instructions, and learned everything Reto had to teach, he would someday be bringing in a million dollars a year or more. It took Kyle a lot of hard work and diligence, but five years later, he got there and stayed there.

It wasn't easy, and success doesn't come overnight. He read all the books given him to read, learned our processes, did demos, knocked on doors. He took it seriously and now he is one of the top professionals in the field.

We all have things of value to share. Surround yourself with people that can teach you things, people you want to be like, and you will find your mentors.

If you want to be mentored by a top-flight lighting professional, you need to attend a dealer congress and apply.

Our Mentorship Program

Mentorship program requirements.

We are very excited, honored, and extremely pleased to announce the addition of a special new mentoring program we've established. We are offering 5 participants the opportunity to get hand-selected for this program. We'll provide each of the 5 nominees who are selected with an extremely generous and beneficial mentorship program that can provide those folks with the keys to unrivaled success.

This new program provides robust techniques like nothing else that has been offered to aspiring business owners before. We want to lead the way in providing a solid network of complete turn-key solutions that will continue to pay it forward, year after year. We truly value hard work and innovations, and we want to reward and empower people who have a strong will to succeed. We know we can create the most valuable selection of dealers and products this nation has seen, through real, hands-on, mentoring.

To completely understand the value and benefits of this program, we suggest you call us to discuss the details further. Note that you must attend our Dealer Congress event to enroll in this life-changing opportunity, and we are seeking people that fully understand what it means to be mentored and will take it seriously.

There is no sense in getting a mentor if you're going to hold back or not fully commit to whatever mentorship program you choose. Does everyone need a mentor? You betcha. Will everyone seek one out? Not likely.

But getting a mentor, choosing a mentorship program that feels like the right fit for you, is just the beginning. That's when the real work begins. Don't waste your money or your mentors time if you're not going to trust them and do what is asked of you.

It's pointless!

We value our Dealers like no other company in the lighting industry, and we would like nothing more than to create more success stories. It's why we do what we do. Our team of experts has been coordinated by experienced leaders in the LED lighting space to share and enable the keys for success with our mentees and help them grow their businesses as fast and as painlessly as possible. We have decades of perfected strategies to share with people that are willing to do the hard work.

At Garden Light LED, we've thought long and hard through decades of experience to really understand how this model can truly transform anyone's life. We enable people to grow a multi-million-dollar business from scratch in this fast-growing LED lighting industry by harnessing our methodologies.

Ask yourself, would you like to join a program that can accelerate you and your team into a very successful LED lighting business? You don't need to be a lighting professional; you don't need to have ever worked as an electrician or installer. Guess what; you don't even need to be a successful business planner or entrepreneur to join and strike it rich. Why? Because we are going to share our greatest assets and knowledge of the industry with you, but only if you can see the vision of where you can take this. Our mentees have to see their future as bigger than it is at present. They must want to scale up, to add staff, project managers, install teams. They must be willing to do the nighttime demos and show clients what they're capable of.

All the mentoring in the world will not teach you as much as doing the work will. We will show you how to do the work, do the demos, get the jobs, and grow, grow, grow, but only if you have that same vision for yourself. We can't have that vision for you, without you.

Still interested?

Mentoring Program Information

The word mentoring comes from a Greek word meaning enduring. Although mentoring is a common practice for professionals, a formalized mentoring program can create solid structures and effective practices. It's more than just seeking advice one-on-one. It's being part of a complete program, styled for your industry.

Today, professionals seek personal contact with senior members of their industry more than ever before. This kind of relationship provides opportunities for effective feedback and two-way communication and can promote the development of emerging professionals. Our plan is to provide access to experienced professionals in the LED lighting design business who can assist with lighting industry knowledge and career development for mentees that are willing to do the work.

Requirements for Becoming a Mentor

- Be a person with a minimum of five (5) years of experience in the lighting industry
- Commit to a two (2) year term of program participation
- Be accessible by phone and Internet and in person, when possible, to answer questions about the lighting industry
- Share ideas for program improvements and resources for future mentors

Requirements for Mentees:

- Be a person with less than five (5) years of experience in the lighting industry
- Share ideas with the Mentoring Program Committee for program improvements
- Strive to become a future mentor for GLLED Mentoring Program

Chapter 16

Becoming a Master Dealer

When you have a one-to-one relationship with a manufacturer that has a vested interest in your success, you're far more likely to succeed. That company is going to teach you a ton and expose you to everything they know about the industry. You're going to learn what to do and what not to do.

Why do you think people buy franchises? They're turnkey. Everything is laid out for them and tied up in a neat little bow. They get training, training and more training. Why does the franchise itself train the heck out of the new franchise owner? They have a vested interest. Yes, there are big fees attached to owning a McDonalds. They like collecting those fees, for sure. But do you know what they like even more? Collecting all the money, day after day, week after week, from that franchise owner.

When was the last time you saw a McDonalds close? Probably never. McDonalds wants you to succeed. They are a vertical company. They make everything that goes into their stores from the paper goods to the bread to owning the cows that the meat and dairy products come from. The only thing they don't make is the soda, but they have a relationship with the people that do.

If you fail, they lose.

So how does that apply to us?

If you want to own a new business or extend the one you have and become a full-service LED lighting company, you don't have to buy a franchise. We don't need you to pay us a franchise fee or build out a facility. You can start on a shoe string budget, but you do have to do a whole lot of other things. And, if you do all those things, things we've been talking about and that I will reiterate in a minute, what we want is for you to buy our products. Lots and lots of them. Our most successful prodigies have gone through our Master Dealer program, did what we told them to do and are some of the most successful people in the industry today. They buy millions of dollars-worth of our product yearly.

We want to build many more just like them and we are doing just that.

The Four Steps to Getting Involved

So that brings us to the nuts and bolts of our Master Dealer Program.

Let's look at the four steps to getting involved.

1. Attend our Dealer Congress
2. Determine if you are eligible for the program and apply.

3. Be accepted into the program

4. Go through our intense training

Once you've done all that, you will have your foot on the first rung of the ladder to building your LED Lighting Design company.

Let's go step by step:

1. Attend our Dealer Congress

What is the Dealer Congress? Why should you attend?

The Garden Light LED Dealer Congress happens each winter in sunny Florida. It's 2 days of complete immersion into the world of LED lighting.

Day one starts with breakfast at 7:15 am for a jam-packed day full of phenomenal talks on strategies, digital marketing, new technologies and techniques. As the day starts to wrap up, you will learn about lighting demos and be able to play in our Design and Installation Playground where we will enjoy Happy Hour followed by a group dinner. Drop into bed afterwards and get some rest because we're just getting started.

Day two, we are back at it for breakfast at 7:15, after which you will break into smaller groups and rotate through to meet with each of our speakers in small group settings. You'll be able to ask questions and rub elbows with these folks. I can't tell you how valuable these sessions are. The connections you will make can be life changing. After everyone has made these rounds we end the congress with a tour of Garden Light LED's facility. You will get to see our manufacturing process, meet our team and see for yourself the quality of our fixtures.

We finally adjourn at 5:30 pm and you will find that, though exhausted, you're also exhilarated and excited about your future in the business.

In these two days, you will have learned more than you could ever have imagined, been inspired by some of the most successful entrepreneurs you will ever meet and will be ready to decide if the Master Dealer Program is right for you.

The program

Learning Objectives:

- Work with American entrepreneur moguls such as KEVIN HARRINGTON, original Shark from "Shark Tank"

- Become one of the most highly-valued and highly-paid LED lighting professionals in your local market

- Reach your business' peak performance with a roadmap that has been paved for over twenty-one years

- Attend breakaway strategy sessions with the most successful entrepreneurs in the LED lighting industry

- Gain insight on effective leadership, grow with other impactful industry persons of influence and adapt business success through education

- Learn how to own your client, build referrals, and attract the right customers that are profitable and fun to work with

- Perfect Your Pitch, convey Clarity, Credibility, the Problems You Solve, your Company's essence, and "The Why"

- Become the educator– Master LED Lighting technologies and how they relate to the products you sell

- Experience real-time tactical design to deliver installations that outshine your competitors

Program Highlights:

- Build a massive LED Lighting Brand in your local market with high quality American-Made LED Lighting, comprehensive training and digital marketing strategies

- Be customer centric; how to gain, keep and receive referrals from your customers

- All attendees will put their minds together in hands-on training workshops. These real-time applications will ensure that your products and services are second to none

- High-Level techniques to be A CLOSER. Money in the Bank

- Guided tour of the GLLED facility. In our factory, you will see the meticulous manufacturing process first-hand

- Breakaway strategy sessions that will change your business

2. Determine if you are eligible for the program and apply.

We have an application on our website at GardenLightLED.com, if you want to get the ball rolling. Before you do that, here are the things you need to be aware of regarding eligibility.

Eligibility Criteria
- 3 Years in business
- Scan of business license and reseller number
- 3 Years of experience as a lighting designer
- Track record for achieving customer satisfaction
- Knowledge of general outdoor LED product specifications
- Installation competency
- Good Credit history
- Reseller to dealers, architects and specifiers

Formal Application (info requested)
- Years in business
- Principal's names and contact information
- Description of core customers
- Primary geographic area served
- Summary financial information
- Business and personal references
- First year business potential estimate with GL
- Trade show attendance
- Professional association memberships (CLA or ALOP)
- Advanced marketing and lead generation platform

Due Diligence (performed by Sales Rep/Audited by HR)

- D&B report
- Website
- Social media sites
- Industry reference checks
- Personal reference checks

Dealer Benefits

- Right to sell and install a very high quality and dependable LED product
- Excellent technical and warranty support
- Comprehensive product and installation training required
- Specialized access to engineers for technical support
- Sophisticated branding and marketing materials
- Intelligent online order entry
- Logo merchandise store
- Special pricing bundles
- Product and specification sheet downloads
- Photometrics and IES reports
- Comprehensive business development and marketing support
- Formalized training and certification support
- Personalized co-marketed website and eStore
- Dealer Platform onboarding and training
- Geo-targeted digital marketing
- Real-time lead generation and reporting
- KPI results dashboard
- Social presence and reputation management
- Online directory listing standardization

Ongoing Requirements

- Complete application
- Meet eligibility requirements
- Sign Master Dealer Agreement
- Submit 12-month rolling forecast
- Dealer Congress attendance
- Serve on a Master Dealer committee
- Product training certification
- Respond to sales leads within one business day
- Comply with GLLED product presentation requirements
- Comply with GLLED product installation requirements

3. Be accepted.

Once your application has been reviewed and it is determined that you are a good fit for the program, you will have the opportunity to accept our offer to be part of the Master Dealers program. I have to admit that I would consider you a little crazy to turn us down at this juncture, but this will be your last chance to back out. This program is not for the faint of heart. We openly admit that. Think of this as the point in the movie where the hero sees the warning signs about those that dare enter the forest, do so at their own risk. Also think about the rewards those heroes always glean from making that journey.

4. Go through our intense training.

Once you decide this is something you will take on, the fun really starts. You will join us in Florida for what is basically a boot camp. You'll be assigned to one of our strategic partners who will take you with them on their jobs.

These guys have worked with us for years. We refer them a lot of business and they buy a lot of product because they know the quality of the equipment we make.

You'll get down in the dirt with them and do installations. That's first and foremost. You HAVE to learn to install your lights. You'll set up nighttime demos, go with them to experience their bidding process, and watch how they close the deal. You'll learn about color theory and use of color which fixtures are best for what applications. You'll spend time in our facility learning some of our engineering and manufacturing processes.

> It's hands on experience which is the best way to learn anything.

After all that, we will send one of our guys to work with you in your territory. There will be lots to read, lots to learn, videos to watch but mainly, it's hands on experience which is the best way to learn anything.

The overview of the Master Dealer agreement

Here are the some of the expectations for applicants:

Dealer Responsibilities:

1. Agree to the guiding principles of the GLLED/ Dealer relationship
2. Agree to an exclusive relationship with GLLED for the purchase of all outdoor LED lighting products
3. Know the specification and applications for all products
4. Know and comply with the approved installations for the products

5. Process all GLLED leads within one business day
6. Know the approved GLLED sales process (Needs Identification process)

   a. Ask approved questions to determine the customer's needs
   b. Clearly state the needs back to the customer
   c. Confirm customer agreement with their needs
   d. Match the customer needs to specific product features
   e. Confirm that selected product features meet the customer's needs
   f. If no, present new features
   g. Confirm customer agreement
   h. If yes, close the sale

7. Attend at least one dealer congress per year
8. Participate on at least one of the following committees

   a. Marketing
   b. Product development
   c. Customer service
   d. Training

9. Effective use of all GLLED product samples and marketing materials
10. Submit a rolling 12-month sales forecast
11. Achieve quarterly/annual sales goals

Here are our responsibilities:

GLLED Responsibilities:

1. Establish the Guiding Principles of the GLLED relationship
2. Design and manufacture the most innovative and

highest quality outdoor LED lights in the industry.
3. Design, manufacture, and offer the most innovative installation peripherals in the industry, such as transformers, connectors, wire etc.
4. Customer service
5. Marketing & market development
6. High quality lead generation
7. Customer conversion training
8. Quality marketing collaterals
9. Online ordering/Inventory availability
10. Comprehensive product, installation, and business development training
11. Provide sales history
12. Provide sales forecast template

Training Segments

1. Customer Experience
2. Product review and capabilities
3. Design potential
4. Installation

Customer Experience

1. Spirit of excellence
2. Best installation, spotless
3. Incredible design
4. Tailored and exclusive experience to the homeowner
5. Professionalism
6. Collared shirts – Cache pants, no logos
7. Don't park in drive way
8. Vehicle spotless and personal hygiene excellent
9. Never go into homeowners house or eat their food

10. Do not eat, drink or smoke on the jobsite

Product Review

1. Understanding the technology
2. Application
3. Opportunities and capabilities
4. Differentiators

Design

1. Proper usage of product
2. Architectural
3. Perimeter
4. Landscape
5. Unique applications
6. Tricks and solutions
7. Ambiance
8. Layering of light
9. Project plans

Installation

1. Transformer selection
2. Lurton formula
3. Series selection
4. Driver calculation
5. Wiring power supply
6. Calculating watts
7. Watts per run
8. Gas tight drum connectors
9. Non-corrosive wire
10. Core drill
11. Unusual installation

I think by now you should realize just how passionate I am about this program. I feel this way because I created it and I am working to develop and execute it day in and day out. I work with installers, Master Dealers and manufacturer reps to make introductions and provide new value to businesses and end users. It's everything to me.

No one has ever created this strategy; connected all the dots. The Master Dealer, Designer Installer component is the commodity. The digital marketing piece of the puzzle brings us into today's reality and extends into the future. I know we all need to embrace it. I love being able to put it all together.

You can make beautiful lights and we do. But, if you have no one to install them, they're lights under a bushel.

Our Master Dealers are our strategic partners. Our team is our extended family. They make us shine. I hope more of you join us and shine with us as well.

Don't hide *your light* under a bushel!

Acknowledgements

I would like to dedicate this book to my husband Reto and our four children. The day I met Reto I knew somehow my life would never be the same. We fell in love, decided to marry and work together very quickly. I had a hunch we'd make amazing business partners; be the "What and the Why" for one another.

When it comes to business, Reto and I have successfully worked side-by-side for over 18 years. His brilliant mind, many years of lighting experience and entrepreneurship have proven to be a first-hand education. He offers his unparalleled insight, which is instrumental in my business development and the development of others. Reto is "A GREAT AMERICAN ENTREPRENEUR"

Special tribute to Heidy and Eugene Mueller for literally spending months on weekend cook-a-thons to teach me generations of family recipes. Reto, thank you for sharing your family and beautiful Switzerland with me. We have created unforgettable memories and shared incredible moments with Elizabeth Weber (Mumeli) and Fritz Weber (Fatu), Fritz and Romy Weber and your brothers Dominic and Claudio Weber.

Number 1 - thank-you for being such a great teacher. Your strong personality, intelligent mind and unwillingness to compromise attitude, fuel Dad's and my desire to provide a foundation that we did not have. You've helped me learn to hope, dream, love, and sacrifice and forgive on-levels I didn't even know existed. Your character and qualities will be the foundation to fulfill your dreams of becoming one of the best attorneys in the nation.

Number 2 - teachers, friends and family have referred to you as an idealist. You are destined for greatness, and Dad and I are grateful that we are the lucky ones chosen to help you develop and grow. Your spirit and presence make the world a better place. I refer to you as an American Entrepreneur even at your young age.

Number 3 - your imagination is profound and inspiring. You are by far the funniest in the family. You have the gift of intelligence and humor. I seriously believe you are going to invent something that solves people's problems. At a young age, you intricately built, engineered, and created opportunities with you mind and heart. I appreciate all the marketing intelligence and support you have provided to Dad and I. Who knows, maybe a marketing guru in the making.

Number 4 - your ethereal soul is inspiring, and the world needs people like you. You are the artist of the family; watching baking shows and creating recipes for the house to enjoy is one of the many perks of your existence. Thank you for cleaning and scrubbing down the kitchen regularly, you take after Daddy. You have a voice like an angel and bring peace and tranquility to our environment.

Kevin Harrington – Friend and mentor

Topher Morrison – Thanks for convincing me to join KPI X. I never would have written this book. So, thank you!

Eli Gonzalez – So glad to have met you through Topher. You and your team have helped me out tremendously!

Lil Barcaski – This book would not be what it is without you. I'm thankful for your gift and your time.

The Garden Light LED family

For believing, dedicating and investing your time in Reto and I, the team and our customers.

Our marketing team - Jason Swilley and Casey Alonso, my angels who came to my rescue.

Marcel Babers – Thanks for teaching me the difference between marketing and P.R.

Cory Glenn – LED Artistry installation chapter.

Rob Singer – Lite It Up.

Rene Morris – Thanks for your decades of support and love. You are a huge part of the success of Garden Light.

Doug Santoro – Doug thank you for being a "Rock" in the organization.

You have a wonderful way of always supporting others and bringing out their full potential.

Luis Couttolenc – You are an amazing partner who has tread new and completely unknown and unchartered waters with me for decades and I love you for that.

Jeanette Gonzalez and Mario Casillas, thank you for believing in and carrying out the Master Dealer Program.

Alfred George Singer – Rob Singer's dad who taught Reto to sell lighting.

My Friends

My Mentors

Our Customers

Thank you for supporting and challenging Garden Light LED to deliver the best!!! You are very important to us and at the center of everything we do!

Last but not least – **my Mom** for believing in me, supporting me and putting up with my younger, imperfect self. You've taught me everything I know. I would not be the person I am today without you.

And also, my grandfather Howard Dietzel who taught me everything I know in sales, marketing, and relationships. This man was truly my best friend and greatest mentor.

Thanks be to God for all that you are in Reto's and my life. You show yourself in every way, we praise you for your blessings and honor you in all that we do.

You have blessed us with a beautiful family and a wonderful extended family through Garden Light LED.

Garden Light LED was built upon

Proverbs 11:25

"By water others you water yourself"

Michelle Charles - Mueller – Biography

Chief Strategist of Garden Light LED

Born and raised in Detroit, Michigan, Michelle is married and has four children with her life and business partner Reto Mueller. Michelle has a 22 - year track record for driving revenue and profit growth through innovative marketing, sales, and branding strategies. Her specialties include team building, and leading groups to their desired organizational goals. Consistently throughout her career, she has proven to design and implement profit-generating business models.

Michelle is the co-founder of a US-based, internationally renowned, LED landscape lighting manufacturing company. *Garden Light LED* is a Tampa-based designer, engineer and manufacturer of high-quality architectural and outdoor LED lighting. Over the past 21-years, *Garden Light LED* has provided lighting solutions and systems for millions worldwide and is recognized for its ingenuity and CNC machined quality products.

Michelle has worked with hundreds of American Entrepreneurs throughout North American, 30 of which have generated multi-million lighting businesses. The company has transitioned from a reseller to an enterprise that combines industrial and digital design and next generation LED technology. *Garden Light LED* is committed to building their partners businesses by offering their unique **Master Dealer Program.**

Recommended reading

Think and Grow Rich
– by Napoleon Hill

E-Myth
– by Michael Geber

Business Success Through Self-knowledge –
by William D. Anton PhD

Ascend
– by William D. Anton PhD

Start with Why
– by Simon Sinek

Leaders Eat Last
– by Simon Sinek

Good Profit
– by Charles G. Koch

Good to Great
– by Jim Collins

Blue Ocean Strategy
– by W. Chan Kim and Renée Mauborgne

Leading the Field
– *by Earl Nightingale*

The Shack
– *by William P. Young*

The Other 90%
- *by Robert K. Cooper, PH. D.*

Get Out of Your Own Way
– *by Robert K. Cooper, PH. D.*

12 Rules for Life
– *by Jordon B. Peterson*

Psycho - Cybernetics
– *by Maxwell Maltz*

Everybody Matters
– *by Bob Chapman and Raj Sisodia*

Return on Character
– *by Fred Kiel*

The 4 Disciplines of Execution
– *by Sean Covey and Chris McChesney*

The Fifth Discipline
– *by Peter M. Senge*

Difficult Conversation
– *by Douglas Stone and Bruce Patton*

Emotional Intelligence
– *by Daniel Goldman*

Altered Traits
– *by Daniel Goldman and Richard J. Davidson*

The Brain that Changes Itself
– *by Norman Doidge, M.D.*

Finding and Keep the Love You Want
– *by Harville Hendricks, PH. D*

How not to Suck at Sales
– by Jeffrey Gitomer

Be Obsessed or BE Average
– by Grant Cardone

The Dip
– by Seth Godin